MW00423411

A Spiritual Guide through Pregnancy

Margaret L. Hammer

Augsburg
MINNEAPOLIS

A SPIRITUAL GUIDE THROUGH PREGNANCY

Copyright © 1997 Augsburg Fortress. All rights reserved. Except for brief quotations in critical articles or reviews, no part of this book may be reproduced in any manner without prior written permission from the publisher. Write to: Permissions, Augsburg Fortress, Box 1209, Minneapolis, MN 55440.

Scripture quotations are from the New Revised Standard Version Bible, copyright © 1946, 1952, 1971 by the division of Christian Education and the National Council of the Churches of Christ in the U.S.A. Used by permission.

Cover design by Elizabeth Boyce
Text design by James Satter

Library of Congress Cataloging-in-Publication Data

Hammer, Margaret L.
A spiritual guide through pregnancy / Margaret L. Hammer.
p. cm.
Includes bibliographical references.
ISBN 0-8066-3344-1 (alk. paper)
1. Pregnant women—Prayer-books and devotions—English.
2. Mothers—Prayer-books and devotions—English. I. Title.
BV4847.H35 1997
242'.6431—dc21 97-18430
CIP

The paper used in this publication meets the minimum requirements of American National Standard for Information Sciences—Permanence of Paper for Printed Library Materials, ANSI Z329.48-1984.
∞

Manufactured in the U.S.A. AF 9-3344

01 00 99 98 97 1 2 3 4 5 6 7 8 9 10

Contents

Introduction

What does it mean to carry a child within your womb? What will bringing a new child into the world mean for you and your way of life? When I was pregnant I devoured books on pregnancy—I wanted to know everything that was going on within me and what I could expect. What was happening with the budding guest in my womb this week? What kind of food should I eat; what kind of exercises should I do? Where should I plan to give birth; whom should I choose to help me deliver? Would it hurt a lot; what could I do to prepare? I listened with mixed feelings to the birthing stories of friends. I dreamed dreams. I prayed a lot.

The mixed feelings, dreams, and prayers all point to the spiritual dimension of pregnancy and childbirth. This time in a woman's life presents spiritual as well as physical challenges—we are, after all, more than a bundle of biological processes. A pregnant woman faces dramatic changes in body chemistry and shape, the challenge of the upcoming birth, and the new responsibilities that will follow. Within the course of a few months, her spirit labors to comprehend it all. No wonder pregnant and postpartum women experience more mood swings than usual!

Yet I didn't find much in the course of my reading that focused on the spiritual adventure of pregnancy and childbirth. Since my first search for guides to pregnancy, I have given birth to three children, ministered and talked to many women in the course of my work as pastor, and researched childbirth literature for my book *Giving Birth: Reclaiming Biblical Metaphor for Pastoral Practice.* I am more convinced than ever that the childbearing year offers vital opportunities for spiritual growth. Neglecting these opportunities is as foolish as neglecting to have a proper diet during pregnancy.

The meditations in this book offer my reflections on samples of the Bible's food for the soul. You will find the meditations grouped in ten thematic chapters. These ten chapters have been arranged to correspond loosely to the nine months of pregnancy and first month after birth. Read them in order, month by month, or skip around and explore as the spirit moves you. Some women start thinking about how they will cope with birth pangs very early on. If you're one of them, go ahead and read some of the meditations in chapters seven or nine. On the other hand, you might want to save some of chapter three's exploration of your feelings about your body's changing shape. I put this chapter early in the book, because you will probably start watching for and thinking about the changes going on in your body right away. The changes will keep coming though, and the last few meditations might help you better later. Feel free to use the book to suit your own needs. Each chapter, indeed each meditation, can stand on its own.

Each meditation begins with a verse or two from the Bible and concludes with a short prayer and questions for reflection. Read the meditations as part of your personal devotions or use them to prime the pump of your own thoughts and musings for your journal. If you do not already keep a journal, now is a good time to give it a try. Whether you use a spiral notebook or invest in a beautifully bound book with blank pages, take time to record your thoughts and feelings, your dreams, your hopes and fears. Try to figure out what you are experiencing, try to discern God's hand in it all. Even if the handwriting is hasty or the spelling imperfect, your journal will be a precious reminder of this special time in your life, and it may help you see patterns you would otherwise miss.

Feel free to share the book's meditations and your responses to them with your husband or a friend. The meditations and questions for reflection can also serve as discussion starters among pregnant friends or in a prenatal support group. If you want to explore some of the issues raised here in greater depth, you can find help in the suggestions for further reading at the back of the book.

For many of us, pregnancy is both the time when we feel most governed by our biology, and a time when we feel especially attuned to life's mysteries and the meaning of it all. Curiously enough, pregnancy's dramatic physical changes seem to make us especially open to the movement of the spirit. Enjoy the opportunity!

1

Expecting a Blessing

"So God created humankind in his image, in the image of God he created them; male and female he created them. God blessed them, and God said to them, "Be fruitful and multiply . . ."
—Genesis 1:27 f.

Congratulations! You and your mate have been blessed! Deep inside you a miracle has begun. Hundreds of millions of tiny sperm raced to unite with your ripe little speck of an egg. One of those millions came first and joined with your egg. Together they became the beginning of a completely new person. Before you knew it, that bud of a person had nestled itself into the rich lining of your womb. In the course of a few months, that tiny speck will grow into a fully formed baby who weighs several pounds and can survive outside your womb. What a miracle!

When we fall in love and have babies, we play our part in the great creation story God started so many generations ago. The very first chapter of the Bible tells us how God blessed birds and bees, flowers and trees, fish and land animals. God gave them all the ability to be fruitful and multiply. Then God turned to humankind—and blessed us, too. God gave us our sexual drives and our ability to have children so that we could fill the earth. What an honor to take part in such a glorious ongoing production!

Not everyone would agree that childbearing is such a blessing. Some ancient myths describe sex and family as chains that the gods use to enslave people and prevent them from reaching too high. Even today, you may know people who view pregnancy as punishment for having sex. Some people fear marriage as a trap and don't want children to come and mess up their lifestyle.

Children do change their parents' lifestyles. Your child will lay claim to your love and attention. Changing diapers and playing "peekaboo" are only the beginning. Still, the joys far outweigh the sacrifices. You can look forward to your child's first smile, her first step, his first word, and the wonderful unfolding of his or her personality. As our three youngsters recently exclaimed, almost as one: "What would you do without us?"

What would we do without our children? We are indeed blessed. The Bible makes that clear from the very beginning: the ability to bring children into the world is an important, God-given blessing. Right after putting human beings on the scene, God looked out over the fertile, newly created world and all its multiplying creatures. Just imagine the hormones that must have been bubbling through the air—rabbits chasing each other, humans embracing, chicks hatching, and flowers blooming. Without a moment's hesitation, God put the divine seal of approval on all of it: "Very good, very good indeed."

You and your mate are indeed blessed. What a blessing to pass life on to your children! What a miracle to see your love take form in a unique new person! What a soul-stretching blessing to share your lives with this new child of your love!

Dear God, thank you for blessing us with the ability to have babies. Thank you for creating us so that our lovemaking can blossom into a whole new person. Help us to enjoy these blessings and to take good care of the children you give us. Amen.

✦ Do you think of childbearing as a blessing, a nuisance, a duty, a luxury, or something else? What do you base your views on?

"God blessed them, and God said to them, "Be fruitful and multiply, and fill the earth and subdue it; and have dominion over the fish of the sea and over the birds of the air and over every living thing that moves upon the earth."
—Genesis 1:28

"You sure are fruitful," my friend said. I had just told her that my husband and I were expecting our third child. Was her remark a compliment or a criticism, or a little of both?

If you already have children, you may find that some people will raise their eyebrows when they learn that you are pregnant again. We don't hear quite as much about the "population bomb" today as we did a few years ago. Still, we all know that the world we live in is not as new and empty as it once was. Indeed, some people would argue that God's command to fill the earth is outdated. They worry that our earth is already full to overflowing.

Perhaps you gave these matters some thought even before trying for your first child. After all, God didn't just say, "Fill the earth," and leave it at that. God also said, "Tame the earth, and rule the animals." God calls us to fill the earth *and* to manage it and its creatures wisely. Today, more than ever, these two jobs seem to pull in opposite directions. For example, in the city where I live tall trees fall again and again to the chain saw, and condominiums and shopping centers spring up in their place. When we cut down forests to make homes for ourselves, we force out the deer and bears and eagles who lived there before. We may gain some jobs, but we also lose when we force out our animal neighbors. We lose the refreshing air and beauty of the forest. We lose places for children to build tree houses and search for tadpoles. More and more, we lose touch with nature.

I know a couple who thought about these things and decided not to have any children. That was over fifteen years ago, and they have stuck to their commitment, as well as sticking with each other. I respect that couple's commitment to caring for the earth, but I am sorry the world won't be blessed by the children they might have raised. Those children might have spoken out on behalf of the earth and the animals. Those children might have blessed the world with their values and wisdom.

Bringing children into our broken world will always be an act of hope and courage. It always has been: the world has never been an easy place to live. Each generation faces its own challenges. In the midst of those challenges, remember that you have been blessed. God has blessed you and your mate both with your fruitfulness, and with your minds, hands, and hearts. God has blessed you with the ability to take good care of the world, and God has blessed you with the opportunity to show your children how to do so, too. May the blessing you have received send waves of blessing on down through the generations to come.

Dear God, thank you for blessing us with children to love and teach. Thank you for the lovely world we live in, and for blessing us with the wisdom to take good care of it. Help us live up to the promise of these blessings.

✦ How do you feel about your own fruitfulness? Think of ways you can manage to both provide for your children and care for the earth.

"Isaac prayed to the Lord for his wife, because she was barren; and the Lord granted his prayer, and his wife Rebekah conceived."
—Genesis 25:21

Did you pray that you would get pregnant? Maybe you became pregnant before you had time to pray about it. Or maybe you had been praying that you wouldn't get pregnant and now feel let down. If that is the case, hang in there. God doesn't always answer prayers on our terms—but wait and see, God *does* answer prayer. Maybe, though, you are one of the many women who really wants to get pregnant and then are surprised to find themselves waiting. You wait and pray, and then pray and wait.

How ironic life sometimes seems. You pray for years that you won't get pregnant—at least not just yet. Then finally you decide that the right time has come. You have finished school and perhaps have already established yourself in a career. You have settled into your marriage, and you and your spouse both feel ready to welcome a child into your lives. You quit using contraception and enjoy the freedom of making love without the hassle and worry. Lovemaking takes on new, creative meaning as you start actively hoping that by making love you will make a baby.

You wait eagerly, and you pray. A month goes by, then two and three. Your period keeps coming, regular as clockwork. Four months go by, and even five. The months never seemed so long. Of course five or six months of fruitless trying does not mean that you have a fertility problem. Still, if the months drag on, you and your husband probably find yourselves praying more, as well as trying to schedule your lovemaking better.

When you pray for God's help in getting pregnant, you follow in the footsteps of couples throughout the generations. Isaac prayed that his beloved Rebekah might conceive. Hannah, who was to become the mother of the prophet Samuel, wept and prayed so fervently for a child that the priest thought she must be drunk! (You can read Hannah's story in 1 Samuel 1-2:21.)

Those months of waiting and praying give you a little taste of the feelings endured by people who spend years trying to get pregnant. Hope struggles with disappointment; feelings of helplessness mix with attempts to figure out what's wrong and to solve the problem. The months you waited to get pregnant can open your heart to the pain such couples feel and help you share your joy in a compassionate manner.

Moreover, those months of waiting and praying can help turn our attention to God, the Lord and giver of life. The waiting reminds us that we do not have complete power over our own fertility. We know pretty well how to prevent pregnancy, but we do not know how to make sure that pregnancy will occur. Even flashy modern medical techniques cannot guarantee conception. Expensive, high-tech fertility treatments work sometimes, but not all the time. God remains the giver of life.

Biblical birth stories highlight this very point. Many important women from the Bible struggled with infertility for years before they got pregnant. Sarah, Rebekah, Rachel, even Leah—the four founding mothers of Israel—were all infertile for a time. Hannah, Samson's mother, and Elizabeth also all prayed long and hard for God to open their wombs. Their stories remind even those who get pregnant easily not to take fertility for granted.

Pregnancy is a gift of God—although if you didn't want this pregnancy you may have a hard time seeing it that way right now. Passing on the gift of life is a great privilege, even when your circumstances are less than ideal. The words of Martin Luther remind us to respect the miracle of childbirth. He once wrote that a woman in childbirth can boast that what she is doing is pleasing in God's sight—even if her child is born out of wedlock. What a strong affirmation—especially when you remember that Luther lived in a society that had little tolerance for pregnancy and birth outside of marriage.

Pregnancy is a gift of God every time—whether you prayed for it or not, whether this pregnancy comes at a convenient time or not, whether you received medical help in conceiving or not.

Dear God, thank you for listening to our prayers. Thank you for giving us what is good for us, even when we don't know enough to ask for it. Thank you for the gift of this pregnancy; help me rejoice in it. Stay near me these next months, and help my baby grow healthy and strong.

✦ Do you think prayer has influenced your pregnancy? If so, how?

"The Lord said to Abraham, 'Why did Sarah laugh, and say, 'Shall I indeed bear a child, now that I am old?'"
—Genesis 18:13

Can you believe it? You're really pregnant! So little seems to change during the first few weeks of pregnancy. You don't look any different. You may not feel any different. An overdue period may make you wonder, but it doesn't prove that you are pregnant. Even when a doctor tells you that your pregnancy test came back positive, the whole thing may seem a little unreal: "Who, me—pregnant?"

The first signs are so slight. Your head and heart may need time to take in what your belly already holds. Believe it or not, when I was pregnant for the first time, I welcomed even the nausea I felt at the smell of coffee. Here was gut-level proof that what the midwife had told me was true. I was indeed pregnant! I must admit that the nausea soon lost its charm, but fortunately it also soon wore off. By then, my body had begun telling me in many other ways that this pregnancy was for real. My breasts were plumping out, my waist was thickening. I had never watched my body so closely.

Whether this is your first pregnancy or whether you have been through it all before, you may go through a whole range of feelings as you watch your body for signs. One moment you may laugh with joy and wondering disbelief like Sarah. The next moment you may feel scared, sad, or even angry, and wish that you had your predictable old body back.

Whatever your particular mix of emotions, accept them and explore them. "Why did Sarah laugh?" the Lord asked. Seems like a foolish question, doesn't it? What ninety-year-old woman wouldn't laugh if some stranger predicted that she would soon bear a child—especially if she had been barren all her life? Abraham had fallen on his face laughing when God had told him the news (Genesis 17:16).

Still, we can learn something about the workings of the human soul if we stop to ask why Sarah laughed. Did she think the stranger was making fun of her? Did she laugh out of disbelief? Or was it to protect herself from yet another disappointment? Did she laugh out of an absurd hope that had already begun to take root in her heart?

When the Lord asked Sarah why she laughed, she denied that she had done so. She didn't dare admit her wild jumble of feelings—her disbelief, her hope, and her fear of disappointment. The Lord didn't punish Sarah, though, either for her disbelief or for her denial. Instead, the Lord's parting words to Sarah corrected her and put her on the path to greater self-understanding: "Oh yes, you did laugh."

Explore your feelings, the negative as well as the positive. Take them all to the Lord in prayer. Doing so will help you make room in your mind and heart for the child who has already begun to develop in your womb.

Enjoy these first weeks, as you watch for your belly to blossom and give you unmistakable proof of your pregnancy. For me, these eager weeks of watching give a good picture of the Christian life. Like Sarah, Christians have received God's promise of blessing beyond our wildest imaginations. Like Sarah, we wonder and hope. We long for clear evidence to show that God's promise has begun developing within us. So, as an expecting mother watches for signs to confirm her pregnancy, we watch throughout our lives for signs of God's presence to confirm our spiritual pregnancy. And as the Christ child grows in our hearts, that spiritual pregnancy will surely show.

O Lord, some days I just can't believe this is really happening to me. Sometimes I wonder if everything is working correctly inside me. Sometimes I shiver with the sheer wonder of it all and can't sort out all my feelings. Help me accept all the new things happening deep within me. Help me open my heart to the child already snuggling in my womb. Help me trust in your loving care.

✦ What changes have you noticed in your body? How do you feel about them? Try to imagine Christ growing in your soul, like your baby grows in your womb. What signs of this "spiritual pregnancy" can you see in your own life and in the life of others?

"After those days his wife Elizabeth conceived, and for five months she remained in seclusion [After the angel Gabriel's visit], Mary set out and went with haste to a Judean town in the hill country, where she entered the house of Zechariah and greeted Elizabeth."
—Luke 1:24, 39-40

You have just learned that you carry a tiny bud of a child deep within you. Whom do you tell, and when?

Some women can hardly wait to share the news. They rush to tell their husbands, their parents, their friends and colleagues, and their sisters and brothers. I know a woman who was so eager to tell her husband the big news that she drove right through a red light on her way home from the doctor's office!

Other women hold on to their secret. Perhaps their pregnancy comes at a bad time, so they wait for just the right moment to break the news to the baby's father. Or they suspect that pregnancy will affect their position at work, so they put off telling their colleagues. Still others simply feel safer keeping their news close to home until they have made it through the first few risky months of pregnancy.

Maybe you can relate to both ends of the spectrum. The news that you are pregnant is both so wonderful and so intimate. You can tell your family and close friends as soon as you know, and still enjoy carrying a surprise inside as you go about your daily life in an unsuspecting world. You can have fun deciding how to pop your news. You can have fun waiting to see how long it takes for casual acquaintances to notice. (One of my less observant classmates never did notice that I was pregnant. He was sure surprised when I started a new semester with an infant on my arm!)

The way you choose to share your news or keep it close can

give you insight into your personality and your feelings about this pregnancy. Think about the ways you have chosen to share your news. Who were the first people you told, and how did you feel about their responses? Where have you let loose, where have you held back, and why?

Have you been so excited that you couldn't keep the news in, even if you wanted to? If so, you can relate to Jesus' mother, Mary. Mary didn't sit and ponder after the angel Gabriel told her that she would soon bear a special child. She took off at once, hurrying over mountains and plains to see her relative Elizabeth. (I can't help wondering how teenage Mary persuaded her parents to let her drop everything and make such a long trip.)

Mary's pregnancy put her in a dangerous predicament: Pregnancy outside of wedlock was punishable by death in her day and age. Even so, she apparently radiated joy that a savior was about to be born: She didn't even need to tell Elizabeth what the angel had said. As soon as Mary came in and said hello, the child in Elizabeth's womb leapt for joy. At that leap, Elizabeth was filled with the spirit and burst out in words of blessing and joy at Mary's unlikely pregnancy. What a way to have your pregnancy confirmed!

Few of us experience the extremes of joy and danger that Mary did. Still, like Mary, you may find that you simply cannot contain your joy at the miracle underway in your womb—even if it comes as a surprise or at an awkward time.

Perhaps you feel more akin to Elizabeth. Elizabeth rejoiced in her pregnancy, too. Yet she chose to keep her secret for months before giving outsiders the slightest clue. Elizabeth had grown old waiting to bear children. She had learned to put up with her neighbors' careless remarks and their smug attitudes. The years passed and she resigned herself to her infertility. Then she finally became pregnant! What joy—and what a shock to the system! Elizabeth's whole world and self-image were turning upside down and inside out, and she needed some time to grasp the news for herself before she could cope with the neighbors' questions.

Like Elizabeth, you too may need time to adjust to this pregnancy before you go public with it. Maybe you're not quite ready for all the extra attention and well-meaning advice. Holding on to your secret for a while may be the best thing for you to do. Elizabeth's quiet savoring of her joy is just as important to the story as the irrepressible overflowing of Mary's joy.

However you chose to share your news, remember that God will be with you—sharing your joy, giving you courage if you need it, blessing you with sensitivity and tact if you ask for it.

Dear God, you know the secrets of my soul better than I do myself. Help me understand those secrets more each day. Give me courage and a thankful spirit so I can see and rejoice in all the blessings you shower over me. Give me the wisdom and grace to share my joys and hopes and fears with those around me. Amen.

✦ Have you shared news of your pregnancy freely, or have you kept it fairly quiet? What does your way of sharing the news tell you about yourself?

"Then Eli answered, 'Go in peace; the God of Israel grant the petition you have made to him.' And she said, 'Let your servant find favor in your sight.' Then [Hannah] went to her quarters, ate and drank with her husband, and her countenance was no longer sad."
—1 Samuel 1:17 f.

I bought *The Complete Book of Pregnancy and Childbirth* as soon as I got pregnant for the first time. Oh, how I studied that book—

I flipped to the weekly calendar of baby's development much more often than once a week. I poured over drawings of embryos at eight and nine weeks. I waited impatiently from week nine to twelve, so that I could see in the next illustration how my baby had changed. Even a "complete book" just couldn't tell me enough about my baby and about what my body was undergoing.

For many women, the first weeks of pregnancy seem to move so slowly. The month between visits to the midwife or doctor can seem like an eternity. You may wish the time would go faster. Most of us have become used to living at a fast pace. We face "rush hour" on our way to work. We buy fast-food or put something into the microwave if we don't have time to go shopping and cook dinner. We watch news from around the world flit by our TV screens in sound bites and quick images.

You can't rush pregnancy, though. And for good reason: Lots is going on with your baby during these first weeks. Your fertilized egg grows from the size of a tiny speck of dust to the size of a grain of rice in its first three weeks. Two more weeks and it has grown to the size of a lima bean. What's more, that lima bean-sized baby has already begun to look like a human being. If you could look into your womb, you could see its head and arms and legs. By the time you are twelve-weeks pregnant, your baby's little fingers and toes have formed and all its internal organs are in place. All this lively growth and intricate development has been going on inside you—and you didn't have to organize a bit of it! Your body, with God's help, has seen to it all.

For the next few months, you don't have to worry about feeding and clothing your baby. Your body has all that under control. So what do you do with yourself in the meantime? If you are expecting your first child, you may be trying to learn all you can about childbirth and babies—talking with the experienced mothers among your family and friends, paying more attention to other people's babies. If you already have children, you may be thinking about how to introduce a new sibling into the family and how to make room for a new family member.

These next months can also be a time of growth in grace for you. Take the time to wonder at the miracle of life blossoming inside you. Take the time to pray: pray for your baby and all the world's young; pray for yourself and your husband as you start this new chapter in your life together; pray for any children you already have. Take the time to explore your dreams. Many of us dream a lot during pregnancy. Take the time to jot down those dreams and think about them. They may give you fresh insight into hopes and fears that get overlooked in the hustle and bustle of your daily life.

Take this time, too, to meditate on God's word. The meditations in this book can give you a start. Take this time to slow down and set priorities. Take this time to envision yourself as a new mother. You need time to prepare practically and spiritually to receive your new child.

Whatever else you find time for, be sure to enjoy these months of waiting and preparation. If the time seems too long, think of Hannah from the Bible. With only a promise to go on, and before she had even conceived, Hannah rose from her prayers in peace and joyful assurance. Minutes before, Hannah had been weeping her heart out. She prayed that she might get pregnant and vowed that she'd dedicate her child to the Lord—if only she could have one. She had been so miserable, in spite of her loving husband, that she couldn't even eat. Hannah had waited for years, and still had months of waiting ahead of her. Even so, she did go in peace, as the priest Eli said. She left the temple a new woman. She returned to her quarters, ate and drank with her husband, and was sad no longer. So, go in peace. Eat and drink with your husband, and rejoice! Rejoice in these months of waiting, rejoice in the new life to come!

Dear God, give me patience and peace as I wait to see my baby. Help me to rejoice in this time of waiting. Help me fully appreciate this blessed time of being with child. Amen.

✦ Does the waiting time of pregnancy seem long or short to you? What hopes do you have for the next few months?

"Then the woman came and told her husband, 'A man of God came to me, and his appearance was like that of an angel of God, most awe-inspiring; I did not ask him where he came from, and he did not tell me his name; but he said to me, "You shall conceive and bear a son. So then drink no wine or strong drink, and eat nothing unclean, for the boy shall be a Nazirite to God from birth to the day of his death."'"

—Judges 13:6 f.

You have probably heard many stories about pregnant women's unusual eating habits. One woman I know developed a new passion for strawberries. ("I guess it could have been worse," she said as she heaped fresh berries on her plate. "It could have been french fries.") Another woman craved cucumber sandwiches at all hours of the day and night. And then there's the old story about pickles and ice cream . . .

Perhaps you haven't yet experienced the tremendous appetite that shows up by the middle of pregnancy. During the first few months of pregnancy you may have even lost your usual appetite. No matter where you are along the spectrum, chances are that you have begun paying more attention to what you eat and drink. It's one thing to hear that the food and drink you take in will affect your health. ("Yes, I know broccoli is good for me; yes, I do know that chocolate can ruin my complexion.") It's quite another thing to know that you have a baby in your belly who depends on you to eat right and give it a healthy start on life. Suddenly milk and fruit are in, beer and chips are out.

That vulnerable and valuable little person growing in your womb gives you an extra incentive to kick any bad health habits you might have. If you smoke, now's a good time to stop. If you drink too much alcohol and not enough water, now's the time to change. If you sit around too much, now's the time to improve your circulation—find time for a daily walk and some sit-ups.

When athletes prepare for a big race, they pay careful attention to their diet and exercise faithfully according to plan. Often these weeks and months of preparation take on a special atmosphere all their own—the goal of doing well in the race sheds its light over the daily effort of building strong muscles, heart, and lungs. Giving birth is not a competition, of course. Still, your efforts to eat well and exercise wisely can glow with a similar sense of purpose. What a bright goal you are preparing for! In fact you carry your goal with you all the time now. Already you nurture a new individual deep within you. In a few months your baby will be big enough to survive outside your womb. Your body will gather its strength and push your new child out into the world.

The Bible does not say much about diet during pregnancy. One story, though, does tell about a woman who gets special instructions for eating and drinking during her pregnancy. Maybe it's no accident that this woman eventually gave birth to Samson, the biblical hero known for his great strength! An angel told Samson's mother not to eat any unclean food and not to touch any wine or strong drink. Her son was to be a holy man, a Nazirite set apart for God from the day of his birth. By following the angel's instructions, Samson's mother helped set him apart for God even before the day of his birth. As long as he was in her womb, she ate like a Nazirite for him.

Few of us receive dietary instructions from an angel. Still, the care with which you eat, drink, and exercise has spiritual as well as physical importance. The Bible teaches us that our very bodies are God's temple. When you eat and drink good things, you are caring for God's temple in your own body and in the body of your baby.

Enjoy this time of preparation. Savor your food, knowing that it not only builds your own body, but also the body of your baby. Enjoy drinking all those extra glasses of water—imagine the cool, clear water washing away all the waste produced by your body's extra work. Relish the fresh air you draw into your lungs during exercise. All these simple earthly things are vital gifts to your child.

Try doing your exercise and dietary preparations as a couple. Doing so can help you keep your spirits up. It can also give your husband an active role in the unfolding of your family's miracle. Your husband cannot eat for your child as you can, but he can share in your healthy diet and join you on your walks. Some men make a point of giving up alcohol in solidarity with their pregnant wives. Others do more of the cooking than they typically do. Enjoy this time together—talk and plan, breathe in the fresh air and laugh, stretch both your muscles and your heart as you prepare for the birth of your baby.

Dear God, thank you for my body, for my sense of smell and taste, and for my ability to enjoy good food. Lift me up when the thought of food makes me sick. Help me eat wisely and well when my appetite returns and reaches all-time highs. Give me the strength to let go of unhealthy habits. Help me enjoy eating and drinking and exercising for my baby's health. Amen.

✦ Have you changed any habits for the sake of your baby? What do these changes mean to you?

"When Rachel saw that she bore Jacob no children, she envied her sister; and she said to Jacob, 'Give me children, or I shall die!'"
—Genesis 30:1

"Why do most people have two or three children, Mom?"

I took a break from my weeding and looked up into the face of an inquisitive eight-year-old. "Probably because they think two or three is just the right number of children for their family."

"Do you mean people can just *decide* how many children they get?"

Many of us take family planning for granted. But when you stop to think about it, it does seem a little strange. Planning a family, deciding how many children to have and how to space them, sounds so cool and calculating. It sounds like it involves about as much passion as balancing your checkbook. Of course planning is wise, and the decision to raise a family is not to be taken lightly. Still, even the most carefully planned pregnancy remains an affair of the heart and soul as well as of the mind and body. The natural progression of events used to show that relationship more clearly: "First comes love, then comes marriage, then comes Sally with the baby carriage."

Love and marriage no longer lead inevitably to childbearing as they did for our grandmothers. Moreover, the economic advantage children once provided has decreased. Some would even say that having children today is a luxury. Still, couples continue to have children. Indeed, those who cannot conceive will often go to great lengths for the chance to do so. Why? Why do we set our hearts on having children?

There are plenty of reasons, of course. When you bear and raise a child, you contribute a new citizen to your country and to the world. You contribute a new coworker in the gospel to God's kingdom. You give your parents a grandchild to love, and you receive a new person to love yourself. You may want children because all your friends are having children or to keep up with your brothers and sisters. You may want children so you can pass on your family genes, traditions, and name to the next generation. You may want to bear and raise children because you want to experience all that life has to offer; you may want to see if you can really do it. You may see children as a sign of hope in a difficult world. You may simply want to share the life that you love.

I can think of many reasons for wanting to have children, but none of them seems quite complete. Perhaps this is because God has created us with a deep urge to pass on our life and our love. When you ask mountain climbers why they trained and struggled and put their lives on the line just to climb a mountain, they will often answer, "I climbed it because it was there." Bringing children into the world is like that. Our full motivation for desiring children lies ultimately beyond us.

Why did you decide to have a child? Most of us have a combination of reasons—some good, some not so good. We have self-giving and self-affirming reasons, and self-centered ones. Take Rachel, for example. She probably had many good reasons for desiring a child. She and her husband loved each other dearly, and Rachel longed to bear the child of that love. Moreover, Rachel knew that she would need children to support her in her old age. Like most of us, she probably wanted to share her life and love and faith with a child of her own body.

At the same time, there were less healthy aspects to Rachel's fervent desire for children. She was jealous of her sister's fertility. Rachel wasn't content with being her husband's favorite; she wanted to keep up with her sister in the childbearing division, too. Indeed, Rachel's intense desire for children became destructive. Her own life became worthless in her eyes: "Give me children, or I shall die!" she wailed. Her preoccupation with getting pregnant began tearing away at her happy relationship with her husband. He got angry at her desperate demands, and told her in no uncertain terms that he was not to blame.

Rachel finally got pregnant, but only after she had learned to share and cooperate with her sister. So, too, God will help us rise above whatever selfish and destructive motives we might have for wanting children. God will help us love our children for who they are, and not for the advantages they might bring us. God will help us rejoice in the creative potential of our bodies and our love. God will help us rejoice in and live up to the challenges our children bring.

Dear God, thank you for creating us to love one another. Thank you for planting the creative urge deep within our bodies and souls. Help me understand my reasons for wanting a child. Forgive whatever is unworthy in those reasons, and help me care for my child with a right spirit. Amen.

✦ Explore your reasons for wanting a child. What do you expect the child you are carrying to bring into your life?

"Then Mary said, 'Here am I, the servant of the Lord;
let it be with me according to your word.'
Then the angel departed from her."
—Luke 1:38

"Who are you?" my pastor asked us one day during confirmation class. At the time I was twelve or thirteen years old, and I thought this was a pretty weird question. "Who am I? I'm Margaret Hammer." What more could I say?

The pastor must have drawn a lot of blank looks, because he went on to prod us a bit. "Okay, you've got your name, that's a good place to start. You are more than a name, though, aren't you? You're somebody's child. Maybe you're somebody's sister or brother, or somebody's best friend. Maybe you're a math whiz, or a poet, or a great cook. Maybe you're a dreamer, or an entertainer, or an organizer. You're all students, otherwise you wouldn't be sitting here, and you're all baptized children of God."

Who are you? My list has grown and changed over the years. Now I'm not only child and friend, I'm also wife and mother, pastor and writer. Some people say that becoming a mother is the single most important part of a woman's identity. If you feel this way, expecting a child can be both exhilarating and frightening. On the one hand, you know that bearing a child is something that only grown women can do, so this may feel like an entrance into adulthood. On the other hand, you may worry about being overwhelmed by motherhood. Will your own variety of interests and accomplishments get lost in the shuffle of child care and focus on your family?

Mixed feelings are normal. They need not keep you from being a good mother. One scholarly friend of mine was so concerned that motherhood might soften her brain that she prepared a long list of heavy reading to exercise her mental muscles while she nursed her newborn! She plowed through some of it, even though she did eventually slow down and focus on her baby, too. When she realized that her mind didn't automatically turn to mush, she gained confidence and loosened up some. Today she manages to enjoy both her family and her work.

Motherhood need not keep you from developing your own talents and interests. For most of us, motherhood is a lifetime deal; and at first mothering will probably occupy much your time. The labor-intensive end of mothering doesn't last forever, however. Life will go on, and so will you. The God who gave you your special combination of talents will give you opportunities to use and develop them. All you need is the vision, self-discipline, and courage to rise to the occasion.

So where do you get the vision, self-discipline, and courage you will need to balance your life and become the person God intended? I think Jesus' mother Mary can give us a tip. "Nothing will be impossible with God," said the angel who had just delivered the unsettling news that Mary was about to become a mother. Mary took the angel's words straight to heart, and replied with simple courage, faith, and dignity: "Here am I, the servant of the Lord; let it be with me according to your word." Mary accepted God's blessing and the responsibilities that went with it. She accepted it all—the joys and the cares, the danger and the delight, all the uncertainties that now lay before her. In doing so, young Mary realized who she was—a woman who, like the prophets before her, was called to be God's servant.

Most of us are called in less dramatic fashion. Still, in taking up our various callings, we, too, begin to see who we are and who we are intended to become. We find ways to use our skills and share our love. We learn to embrace the future with all its uncertainties. We learn to see a holy purpose in even the most mundane details of daily life.

Dear God, thank you for the talents you have given me, and thank you for blessing me with a baby to love and nurture. Help me to use my gifts wisely and to share my love freely. Give me the vision and the courage to accept the challenges and responsibilities life has in store for me. Amen.

✦ How important do you think motherhood will be to your sense of who you are?

2

Looking for a Caregiver

"Under the apple tree I awakened you.
There your mother was in labor with you;
there she who bore you was in labor."
—Song of Solomon 8:5

What a romantic picture Solomon suggests in these lines about love under the apple tree! Imagine how lovely it could be to give birth in a secluded orchard. You could nestle down in the soft green grass growing in the shade of an old apple tree, lean up against someone you love, and take a deep breath of air scented with the sweet and fresh smells of wildflowers, grasses, and trees. A gentle breeze might caress you as you push. Truly one with nature, you could give birth with birds singing all around you.

Few of us seek so natural a birthing place, however. There might be bees among the apple blossoms, and mosquitoes might be humming along with the singing birds. Mother Nature might provide pouring rain instead of a gentle breeze. Moreover, the attendance of a knowledgeable doctor or midwife can give peace of mind that might be hard to come by out under some secluded apple tree.

Large modern hospitals aim to provide such peace of mind. Their medical staffs keep watch on shifts around the clock. Fetal heart monitors keep close tabs on labor's progress. If problems arise, emergency surgical suites stand ready. The polished and efficient maternity wards of such institutions present quite a contrast to a soft patch of grass under an apple tree.

Which model of birth attracts you most? Some women feel most secure when surrounded by the latest medical technology. Others feel that they can do their birthing work better in a more relaxed, homey environment. Depending on where you live, you may have several birthplace options to consider. Will you feel more confident in a large teaching hospital or in the more relaxed atmosphere of a small community hospital? If you feel strongly about the benefits of a homey environment, you may want to look for a free-standing birthing center in your area, or even plan to give birth in the familiar surroundings of your own home.

Think through your preferences. Gather information from women who have recently given birth in your area. You may want to visit various birthing facilities before deciding which way to go. Whatever your preferences, keep them in mind as you begin looking for a doctor or midwife. Few doctors will assist at home births, and not all midwives have hospital privileges. When you do visit a doctor or midwife, discuss your views on the best birthplace. The more open you are with your hopes and priorities, the better your chances of finding a good fit.

As you think through your options, think too about what your preferences tell you about yourself. Where do you put your faith: in medical technology? in your body's natural capabilities? in skilled attendants? Can you see God at work in all of the above? Your preferences can also tell you where you feel most vulnerable. If you fear that your body will not be able to cope, you will want to be close to medical assistance. If you feel threatened by the foreign routines of the hospital, and the possibility of unwanted medical intervention, you may look into home birth.

Wherever you end up giving birth, rest assured that God will be there with you. There is no apple tree too remote, no hospital room too filled with machines, no taxicab too speedy to keep God from embracing you and your child.

Dear God, thank you for surrounding my baby and me with your love, wherever we are. Help me to find the best birthplace for us both. Give me the courage to share my hopes and concerns with the person I choose to help me through pregnancy and labor. Hold me as I face my fears. Let me go forth confident in your abiding help. Amen.

✦ Imagine your ideal birth setting. Is such a setting available in your community? What does your choice of birth setting tell you about yourself?

"The king of Egypt said to the Hebrew midwives . . . 'When you act as midwives to the Hebrew women, and see them on the birthing stool, if it is a boy kill him; but if it is a girl, she shall live.' But the midwives feared God; they did not do as the king of Egypt commanded them, but they let the boys live."
—Exodus 1:15 ff.

One friend raves about her obstetrician. Another insists that her midwife is tops. A third thinks it makes most sense to stick with your family doctor. The variety of prenatal care options can be confusing. Each of these categories of health-care professionals has its strengths.

Obstetricians are medical doctors who have taken specialized training in the female reproductive system and childbirth. They have considerable experience dealing with complicated pregnancies and births, and they can perform a cesarean section if you need one.

Midwives also specialize in childbirth. Many worked as registered nurses before going through a midwifery program. Others went straight into an accredited school of midwifery. Still others have accumulated their midwifery skills through practical experience. Most midwives emphasize building a strong trusting relationship with you before you have your baby. They use time-tested methods to keep medical interventions to a minimum. A midwife will usually stay with you throughout your entire labor.

Family practice doctors have the medical training to treat your entire family, handling everything from appendicitis to broken bones, from school physicals to childbirth. This means you won't have to go out hunting for a pediatrician shortly after your baby is born. Moreover, it means that you can develop an ongoing relationship with your doctor. The better you know each other, the better health care your doctor will be able to give you. Unfortunately, the rising cost of malpractice insurance has caused some family practice doctors to stop offering maternity care.

What do you look for in the health-care professional you choose to help you through pregnancy and childbirth? Technical expertise is important: I was glad that the obstetrician who performed a cesarean section on me had his technical skills in order. Experience, too, is important: I found it reassuring to hear that my midwife had already helped thousands of babies into the world during her years as a medical missionary. Don't forget wisdom and interpersonal skills either: The caregiver who takes time to get to know you and your values improves her ability to help you make good decisions if your labor runs into problems.

Last but not least, look for a caregiver who fears God. As sixteenth-century bishop Peter Palladius put it when proposing guidelines for the certification of midwives: a midwife should be "competent, enlightened, and God-fearing." This sounds all well and good, but how can you tell if a caregiver fears God?

The story of the Hebrew midwives in Egypt provides a clue. Those midwives showed that they feared God by their courage and their integrity. They remained true to their life-affirming vocation, in spite of the death-dealing powers that threatened them. As far as I know, doctors and midwives don't face such terrible pressure today. Still, they do face plenty of pressure: pressure to keep hospital costs down, pressure to do an extra test or procedure so they can defend themselves if someone decides to sue, pressure to work quickly so they can get on to the next patient. You want to know that the person you choose to help your baby into the world will stand up under these pressures. You want to know that he or she will put the well-being of you and your baby first.

If you have lived in a small town for some time, you may have some sense of the character of the doctors or midwives who practice there. But if you are new in town or live in a large city, you may never have seen your doctor or midwife before you meet at your first prenatal appointment. How, then, can you get a sense of this person's character and competence?

If possible, talk to other women this caregiver has served. (You may need to ask for references.) Did this person prove trustworthy? Did he or she explain things and offer appropriate guidance? Was she available and respectful? Did he display integrity and courage when making difficult decisions?

Moreover, listen to your own intuition. Does this person take time to talk with you and respond respectfully to your concerns? Do you feel comfortable bringing up questions? If something bothers you, look into it until you are satisfied that you have found a caregiver whom you can trust. The efforts you make now will pay big dividends in your peace of mind later.

Finally, pray about your decision. Ask God for guidance; and when you have made your decision, remember to pray regularly for your midwife or doctor. He or she will benefit from your support, just as you will benefit from his or hers.

Dear God, help me find the right doctor or midwife to care for me and the child within me. Give me the courage to ask questions when I have them. Give me the wisdom to sense the character of the person who answers. Bless the work of all obstetricians, midwives, and family doctors. May they always care for people to the best of their abilities and show reverence for you, the giver of life. Amen.

✦ What qualities do you look for in a doctor or midwife?

"When she was in her hard labor, the midwife said to her, 'Do not be afraid; for now you will have another son.'"
—Genesis 35:17

When you see childbirth depicted on television, you usually see a woman writhing and screaming for a few minutes, then out comes a baby. This picture gives a false impression. Real labor doesn't go as quickly as it seems on television. On the other hand, my labors never felt as horrible to me as labor looks and sounds when depicted on TV.

In fact, I think that the hardest part of my own labors was the emotional stress as I waited for contractions to set in. For some reason, my waters always seemed to break long before my womb was ready to swing into action. This meant that I paced maternity wards for hours and even days with the threat of a drug-induced labor or major surgery hanging over my head.

At such times the pastoral skills of your caregiver, as well as their medical competence, mean a lot. I will never forget the midwife who held my hand and prayed with me when she saw how down I felt as the IV equipment rolled into my room. I'll never forget the wise old obstetrician who sat down late one night and explained research pertaining to my situation and encouraged us to wait a little longer before resorting to a cesarean. These women not only knew how birthing bodies work, they also knew how to care for the whole person. They knew how to encourage and strengthen women to face the challenges of labor.

We all need encouragement sometimes—especially when we're stretched to our limits and faced with the unknown. "Fear not," the midwife said to encourage Rachel in her hard labor. The words remind me of angels. "Fear not," the angel said to Mary when he announced she would bear Jesus. "Fear not," the angel said to the shepherds when he announced the birth of the Messiah. Sometimes we need to hear those simple, encouraging words: Fear not. God's angels don't always wear wings and shining clothes. An angel may touch you in the person of an ordinary-looking doctor, nurse, or midwife who encourages you when you need it.

"Fear not," the midwife said, "*for now you will have another son.*" Look for a caregiver who will encourage you and help you see the big picture. People can put up with a lot of pain if they know that it will soon end. People can live through terrible hardships if they have a mission to accomplish: Think of the hardships early explorers, pioneers, and missionaries endured. Martin Luther made a good point when he advised that the best way to comfort and encourage a birthing woman is to remind her that she is doing noble and God-pleasing work. A caregiver who tells you that there is light at the end of the tunnel can bless you with new-found strength and courage. The caregiver who finds ways to remind you that you are doing noble, life-giving work can lift your spirits as you struggle with the ups and downs of pregnancy and the challenges of childbirth.

Look for the angel in your caregiver, and pray that the angel may touch many lives. Pray for all your caregivers—those you know already, and those you may see only for a few hours. Pray that they may be blessed with pastoral sensitivity as well as medical competence. Pray that they may build up the courage and hope of the women they serve. Pray that their eyes may always see the miracle in childbirth, however often they may help a child into the world.

Dear God, help me find a doctor or midwife I can trust. Help me share my hopes and fears with this person; show him or her how to encourage and strengthen me. Thank you for the wisdom and healing power you give doctors and nurses, midwives and pastors. Thank you for calling me to do the noble work of childbearing; give me the grace and courage to do it well.

✦ Can you see angels at work in your life?

". . . and [Ruth] bore a son. Then the women said to Naomi, 'Blessed be the Lord, who has not left you this day without next-of-kin; and may his name be renowned in Israel! He shall be to you a restorer of life and a nourisher of your old age; for your daughter-in-law who loves you, who is more to you than seven sons, has borne him.'"
—Ruth 4:13 ff.

When Ruth gave birth to her son Obed, long before the birth of Christ, her mother-in-law Naomi and a whole chorus of neighborhood women seem to have been on hand. When my mother gave birth to me in the 1950s, only hospital staff people were allowed in labor and delivery rooms. My father got no closer than the waiting room. By the time I gave birth to our children in the 1980s, the pendulum had begun swinging back. Today most hospitals allow you to invite close family members or friends into their birthing rooms. Most birthing centers encourage you to do so.

Think carefully about whom you will invite. Some women want only their baby's father with them. Others invite the baby's grandparents or a close friend or mentor. Some include their older children. Discuss plans early on with your husband. He may be eager to share in the excitement of birthing. Not all men feel comfortable with the idea, though, so don't be too disappointed if he hesitates. For that matter, you yourself may prefer to have a female relative or friend help you. Whatever your thoughts and preferences, talk them through with your husband. Tell him what matters most to you and listen for his feelings. If you really want him by your side in the birthing room and he is still reluctant, encourage him to talk to fathers who have been present at the birth of their children. Sign up for childbirth preparation classes and invite him along.

Whatever your husband ends up doing, make sure that you find at least one person you can trust to stay with you through your birthwork. Such a person can bless your birthing hours in many ways. The mere sight of a familiar face and the sound of a familiar voice can cheer you. A friend's hand to hold can give you new strength. No wonder women who have a companion with them throughout their labor have shorter labors with fewer complications! And if complications do arise, you will want a trusted partner on hand to help you make emergency decisions. In any case, you will appreciate someone willing to pray with you and help you feel God's presence. Last, but far from least, you'll want a friend on hand to help you celebrate when your baby bursts forth on the scene!

Such personal caregivers can make birthing easier by bringing a touch of your home, your faith, and your friends into even the most impersonal facilities. Such persons can also welcome your baby on behalf of all the people who care about you but can't squeeze into the birthing room. Think about the way the neighborhood women received Ruth and her baby so many centuries ago. When little Obed was born, the women thanked God and sketched out how the baby fit into the local scene. They rejoiced in the super strong bonds of love linking Ruth and her mother-in-law, and they voiced the community's hopes for the newborn.

Your baby's birth is an important event in the life of your

community, too. So it's good to have family members or friends on hand. They can help you welcome your newborn. They can give you a well-deserved pat on the back. Finally, as the years go by, they will share memories of your child's birth. I now live miles away from the midwives, doctors, and nurses who helped me give birth to my children. They may not even remember me or the circumstances of my baby's birth. My husband, though, will never forget. Already those birth stories have a special place in our family lore.

Rather than giving birth among strangers, find someone you care for to take part in your birthwork. Whether it be your husband, your sister, your mother, or a friend, ask for the personal care they can best give. Ask them to come pace the floor with you and hold your hand, to tell some stories, say some prayers, surround you with their love, and celebrate a job well done. Take the chance to share the ups and downs of this messy, scary, glorious miracle with people you love.

Dear God, thank you for all the people who love my baby and me. Guide me as I decide whom I should invite to help me during my birthing work. You know the strengths and weaknesses of those I might ask. Help me choose the right people. Give them the courage and wisdom and commitment they will need. Bless us now as we look ahead to my baby's birth. Bless us when I go into labor. Bless us in years to come when we remember these days. Amen.

✦ Who do you hope will be with you when you give birth? Why did you choose this person or persons?

"And Mary remained with [Elizabeth] about three months and then returned to her home. Now the time came for Elizabeth to give birth, and she bore a son."
—Luke 1:56 f.

Two baby girls were born a few days apart, more than fourteen years ago. They have felt a special kind of bond between them ever since. Twenty-eight birthday parties have been celebrated between the two of them now, and neither of them has ever missed a one. Their mothers lived near each other while they were expecting their first babies, and they spent a lot of time walking together and talking together. They both looked forward to the new joys and challenges awaiting them.

A special bond often forms between friends who go through pregnancy at the same time. Pregnant women have so much in common at this exciting time in their lives. No wonder Jesus' mother Mary chose to spend her first months of pregnancy with Elizabeth, an elderly relative who was also pregnant for the first time. They had lots to talk about, and who else could they talk to? Elizabeth's husband had been struck speechless, and Mary didn't have a husband. They would hardly want to talk to their friends and neighbors about their circumstances: Both of their stories sounded pretty wild.

Your pregnancy may have been expected by those who know you. Your circumstances may be as settled and normal as can be. Still, you may feel most comfortable pouring out your thoughts and fears and dreams to someone who's going through the same thing. Your non-pregnant friends will probably show extra interest in how you are feeling at this time. Still, there's a limit to how much pregnancy talk most people who aren't pregnant will find fascinating. On the other hand, when you are pregnant (especially the first time), there may be no limit to your interest in every aspect of pregnancy and childbirth.

If you don't already know women in your situation, try to get acquainted with someone at your childbirth education classes. Ask if your church has pre-birth baptismal classes or support groups for expecting parents. Friendships often bloom quickly in such groups. It's a little like the camaraderie that develops among youths who rent a bus and travel together to a convention, or among mountain climbers who plan for months to take on a mountain together.

Your pregnant friends probably won't be on hand to help you in the birthing room. (Although who knows, you may meet them in the hall!) By the time your contractions get going, some of them may already have plunged into the crazy first weeks of adjusting to a new baby. Others may still be lumbering along, waiting for labor to start. Although these friends may not be physically present with you as you give birth, they certainly can be with you in thought and prayer.

So, too, Mary stayed with her pregnant friend Elizabeth for three months, but then returned to her own home shortly before Elizabeth gave birth. For a few intense months, these two women cared for one another, shared with one another, and helped one another prepare for the future. Then each went her own way, stronger for the time they had spent together and the intimacy that had developed between them. Imagine these two holy women parting: surely they promised to hold one another in prayer as they finished their pregnancies and gave birth to their children.

Similarly, the bonds you form with friends during this time can strengthen you as you take on the challenges of pregnancy, birthing, and new motherhood. The friendships that blossom now may flourish a long time. Think of the two mothers and their fourteen-year-olds that I mentioned earlier. In our mobile world, though, job changes and moves may take you far from one another and make shared birthday parties impractical. Like

Mary and Elizabeth, you may enjoy some intense months together, and then see one another rarely, if at all, as your children grow up.

Whatever the future may bring, pick the flowers of friendship while you can. They will grace your life today and in the wild weeks to come. They will provide beautiful memories to uplift you in the future.

Dear God, thank you for friends. Thank you for people who listen to me and understand what I am going through. Thank you for people who will laugh with me and cry with me, people who will dream with me, challenge me, and comfort me. Thank you, too, for giving me the chance to help my friends. Show us all how to best care for one another, and prompt us to pray for each other. Amen.

✦ With whom do you share your thoughts, questions, and responses to pregnancy? What attracts you to this person or persons?

"My little children, with whom I am again in travail, until Christ be formed in you!"
—Galatians 4:19 (RSV)

"Look, Mom! The father is a lady!" The wide-eyed young boy tugged at his mother's skirt and pointed. He and his Roman Catholic family had just entered a Lutheran church to attend a wedding. He'd been told what to expect and how to behave, but no one had thought to mention that the pastor might be a woman.

Well, I guess a little boy talking about a lady father is no stranger than the apostle Paul referring to himself as a birthing mother. How can a man be a mother? Still Paul chooses to speak of himself as a birthing woman. Why does he do it? When you think about it, you realize that Christians use lots of family language. Some talk about their "church family." Others call church friends "brother" or "sister." Church leaders may be called "Holy Father" or "Mother Superior." This family language reminds us how closely we Christians are knit together in Christ.

Paul takes such family language still further in his letter to the Galatians. There his imagination stretches beyond the limits of his male body. He tells the Galatians that when they fall back into their old, fearful ways, he feels it as deeply and strongly as a mother feels her labor contractions. Like a birthing woman, he struggles to push them on out into the freedom of Christ.

What a wonderful, gut-level picture of a Christian teacher's work! And this birthwork goes on. We, too, struggle to give birth to Christ in our own hearts. We, too, labor to teach and encourage one another, until Christ be formed in every heart.

Look for someone to help you with your spiritual birthwork, especially now as you face so many changes in your life. Your pastor may listen to your joys and concerns and help you see their spiritual dimensions. Even if your pastor happens to be a man, he may well understand something of the highs and lows that pregnant women experience. He may also enjoy learning more about this utterly female experience. One woman asked her pastor and his wife to attend her when she gave birth. The pastor felt uncomfortable about it, so he dragged his feet, hoping to arrive at the hospital too late to witness the birth. Fortunately he got there with time to spare. For weeks afterward he talked and preached about the wonder, suffering, and joy he had the privilege of experiencing.

Pastors are not the only source of spiritual guidance, of course. You may feel more comfortable sharing your thoughts and questions with another woman. If you don't already know someone who fits the bill, ask at your church. The people there may know someone who would enjoy visiting and helping you through pregnancy, birth, and early motherhood. Older women in the congregation often know from experience what you are going through. They may have the time to visit you. What's more, they may have the patience to listen to what's on your mind, and the wisdom to help you put it all in Christian perspective.

The spiritual guide you find may be a lady father, or a travailing male, or a wise older woman. In any case, remember to keep him or her in your prayers. Tending to the spiritual side of pregnancy will be new to most people. Doctors and midwives are trained to chart the changes your body goes through during pregnancy. They use instruments and machines to monitor and measure your physical progress, but they rarely feel free to ask about your spiritual health. Pastors, on the other hand, are trained to teach and preach. They learn about crisis intervention and the stages of grief, but few have studied the spiritual dynamics of pregnancy. Your spiritual guide will probably be exploring new territory right alongside you. Enjoy this opportunity for spiritual growth, and enjoy sharing it with an insightful Christian sister or brother.

Dear God, thank you for giving me thoughts and questions, feelings and dreams, humor and honesty. Help me make sense of the changes that have begun happening inside and around me. Help me find a wise and good person who will listen to me and help my spirit grow while my baby and my belly grow.

✦ Think about Paul travailing to bring Christ to birth in his Galatian friends' hearts. What do you think Paul may have been trying to say with this word picture? Who might help you do your own spiritual birthwork?

"Yet it was you who took me from the womb; you kept me safe on my mother's breast. On you I was cast from my birth, and since my mother bore me you have been my God. Do not be far from me, for trouble is near and there is no one to help."
—Psalm 22:9 ff.

Your waters break weeks before expected, and your midwife or doctor is still on vacation. Yes, they have colleagues who will take call for them, but you had so hoped that the person you knew and trusted would be on hand to attend you. Or your labor starts suddenly, and your husband is miles away, stuck in a traffic jam. No matter how well you choose your caregivers and lay your plans, everything can change at the last minute. You may give birth to your baby surrounded by a whole different crew than you had expected.

Even if that happens, and you feel scared and alone, remember that bad timing will not prevent your most important caregiver from helping you. The psalmist describes God as the Midwife who never leaves her post. God was on hand to catch you the moment you emerged from your mother's womb. God was on hand to protect you at your mother's breast. Ever since those first helpless newborn days, you have been cast on God's breast and sheltered by God's hand. Of course this God will be with you and your baby when you give birth—even if no one else is around to help!

Chances are, though, that plenty of human helpers will be on hand, too. God uses human hands and hearts to accomplish much healing work. Some of the people who touch you with God's presence during your birthing may be people you have never seen before. I will never forget the anesthetist who somehow grasped snatches of the lament I poured out in Danish to my husband. Somehow he leaped the language barrier. He understood me when I said that I felt as if I was stretched out on a cross. He understood my words, and he affirmed my experience. He agreed: "You do feel like you're being stretched out on a cross," he said. He knew what he was talking about. He had once let himself undergo all the preparations for surgery just so he would understand what the people he served were going through.

I had never laid eyes on that man before. We will probably never cross paths again. I don't even know his name. Still, he served as one of God's helping hands that day—both with his technical expertise and with his Christian insight.

Some of the people who touch you with God's presence in your birthing may be people you know well. If your pastor knows you're in labor, he or she may stop in to pray with you. Years after the birth of his child, one young father told his pastor how much a short pastoral visit to the birthing room had meant to him and his wife. "I will always remember how you came and prayed with us. We both knew that God was with us in that hospital room."

Let your church know how you're doing. That way prayer circles can pray for you as you face the challenges of pregnancy and childbirth. Knowing that your church friends are praying for you can give you a real lift, even if you don't hear those prayers yourself. Moreover, prayer makes a healing difference, even when you don't know you're being prayed for. Scientific studies now show what many faithful people have always known: that prayer works. Researchers have begun studying the effects of prayer, using experiments set up according to strict scientific standards. Pastor and journalist Tom Harpur describes such studies in his book, *The Uncommon Touch.* These ground-breaking studies show that prayer has a remarkable healing effect, even among people who don't know that they are being prayed for.

Look for God's helping hands in the world around you. They can bless your pregnancy, your birthing, and your entire life as it unfolds. Troubles may make it hard to see those helping hands some times. Still, even when you feel scared and lonely, God's unseen hands hold you and protect you. God's loving arms will catch you, and bless you, and bring you safely home.

Dear God, help me trust you and lean on you. You were ready at my mother's side when I was born, and you have cared for me ever since. Help me feel you embracing my baby and me right now. Help me see you at work in all the people who care for me. Help me lay all my cares on you and trust you to bring my baby safely into the world. Amen.

✦ Try picturing God as a midwife. What does the picture help you learn about God? Reflect on the ways in which God has protected and helped you through your life.

3

A New Self

"The man named his wife Eve,
because she was the mother of all living."
—Genesis 3:20

"Mom, when does a baby turn into a kid?" What impossible questions children come up with! When *does* an infant leave babyhood behind and enter the ranks of the big girls and boys? For that matter, when does a girl become a woman? When do you become a mother?

Many girls practice mothering in one way or another from an early age on. Maybe you fed and rocked a doll. Maybe you looked after a pet. Maybe you took care of younger brothers or sisters, or earned pocket money caring for other people's children. Even if you have little experience with young children, you may sometimes find yourself mothering your husband or friends.

Maybe, on the other hand, you haven't had much practice mothering. If that is the case, you may feel a little nervous. When big families were commonplace, young girls gained plenty of experience diapering and burping baby sisters and brothers or nieces and nephews. Today, many of us reach adulthood unsure even how to hold a newborn. The chance to hold a tiny child can make a lump of quivering Jell-O out of adults who usually are the picture of self-confidence. That precious little bundle seems so fragile, and no one wants to drop or damage it. No wonder you may sometimes ask yourself, "Will I be able to handle it?" or "How will I know what to do?"

It's all right to feel a little insecure. After all, you have begun a wonderful, challenging adventure. There is plenty to learn along the way. On the other hand, don't lose too much sleep worrying about all the things you don't yet know. Even completely inexperienced women quickly pick up the knack of holding a baby. In no time at all you will become an old pro. As your baby's needs unfold, your abilities will unfold and grow, too. When *do* you become a mother? You might say that you become a mother as soon as you start mothering someone. You might say that you become a mother when you get pregnant or when you give birth. Then again, you might say that you really become a mother when you finally feel comfortable and competent caring for your child.

When *do* you become a mother? My answer is both "already" and "not yet." You are already a mother, regardless of prior experience. Way before the first woman gave birth, even before she got pregnant, her man gave her a name that honored her as the mother of all living. He sensed already that she was destined for great things. She wasn't just his lover; she was the person through whom life would be carried on.

So, too, you were born with mothering abilities that enable you to pass life on into the next generation. You use those abilities every time you comfort or guide someone. You use them every time you feed or shelter someone. Moreover, you have already begun mothering in the most basic sense of the word. You shelter a child deep within you. Your body provides for its every need.

You are already a mother—and yet you still have plenty to learn about mothering. You still have many challenges to face and many joys to discover. No matter how many children you already have, I suspect that you would have to admit that you are not yet the accomplished, gracious, wise mother we all hope to become. None of us are. We do our best, and still we sometimes flub things up. We all stand in need of God's help and forgiveness. As one mother of young children said after a particularly trying day, "I started out intending to be as kind and cheerful as Snow White, and somehow I ended up sounding like the Wicked Witch of the West!"

You are not yet the mother you will become. Remember that on days when you feel discouraged or overwhelmed. Little by little you will learn to mother your infant, your toddler, your school-age child, your teenager. You will learn to respond to your children's wonderfully impossible questions and to learn from them yourself. By the grace of God, you will grow daily in your mothering. With God's help you will pass your life and your love on to your children.

Dear God, thank you for giving me the ability to mother. Thank you for all the people who have mothered me in various ways. Show me how to be a good mother: Help me love forth the best in my child. Forgive me when I fail, and give me what it takes to get up and try again.

✦ Can you picture yourself as a mother? What attracts you to motherhood? What scares you about it?

"Jacob was left alone; and a man wrestled with him until daybreak."
—Genesis 32:24

Have you been dreaming more lately? Many women remember their dreams much more clearly during pregnancy than they usually do. Indeed, some pregnant women find themselves dreaming so much more intensely that they wonder if they're going off the deep end!

Don't worry; all this dreaming is perfectly normal. Maybe the changes in your body's hormone levels give rise to more memorable dreams. Maybe your feelings about all the new things you face simply bubble to the surface when you relax and try to sleep. Whatever the reason, welcome your dreams. Take a look through the window they open into your subconscious.

"Well," you may be thinking, "that is easier said than done. Many of my dreams are scary. I dream about swimming for dear life more often than I dream about playing with a beautiful baby. Who welcomes a scary dream?"

We probably do remember more of our disturbing dreams. After all, they're the ones that usually wake us up! Even scary dreams can tell us important things, though. They may express mixed feelings about being pregnant that your waking self doesn't want to admit. They may express feelings of increased vulnerability now that you carry an extra treasure within you.

What can you do with your dreams? First, keep a notepad by your bed to jot them down before they slip away. Then mull them over during the day and jot down thoughts they bring to mind. Talk them over with your husband or a friend. Some may seem like meaningless jumbles. Others may strike you as particularly significant. Follow the signs and your own intuition. Take care not to avoid the dreams that frighten or bother you. Explore them. What frightens you? Try to figure out how you can face and cope with it. Why does something in a dream bother you? Perhaps your dream will point you toward issues you have been avoiding while awake. Delving into your dreams can be exciting and unsettling. As you do so, pray that the Spirit will help you face and interpret the messages you find.

Interpreting your dreams can give you new insight into your own waking life. It can also give you fresh insight into other symbolic worlds. Take the Bible's story about Jacob struggling through the night with a stranger, for example. Many pregnant women dream at one time or another about being attacked by a stranger. Maybe that is because we feel especially vulnerable at this time in our lives. As pregnancy progresses, our swollen bodies make us clumsier than usual. We are less able to make a quick getaway. At the same time we carry within us a precious treasure that needs our protection.

Moreover, the precious treasure you carry within is also a stranger. This stranger may not be attacking you, but he or she may already have begun keeping you awake at night. Whether due to heartburn in early pregnancy or to baby's stretching and kicking in late pregnancy, we do struggle through the night with a stranger. On a spiritual level, too, we struggle with this stranger within. What will the stranger living in my womb do to my body? For that matter, what will this stranger do to my life? Will this new person mess up my life or bless it—or a little of both?

Such concerns are normal. They don't mean that you won't love your baby. You don't even know your baby yet. For the time being he or she is both a hidden treasure and a totally intimate stranger. It will take time to get used to having this new person in your life.

Exploring your dreams can help you make the most of this spiritual struggle. Focusing on them can help you face things you are otherwise afraid to admit. As you explore your dreams and struggle with your stranger, take strength from the God who knows you better than you know yourself. God will hold you and help you, just as God held and helped Jacob.

Jacob hung on through the night and survived his struggle with the stranger. At daybreak, the stranger gave him a new name and a blessing. So hang on and plumb the depths of those dreams. You, too, will survive the struggle! Soon you, too, will receive a new name. "Mommy" won't replace your given name, but it will mark a new chapter in your life. Jacob came out of his struggle blessed and ready to face a challenging new chapter in his life. You, too, will receive a blessing. The God who holds you through the night will bless and protect you through whatever life may bring.

Dear God, thank you for giving me my dreams. Help me enjoy this time of dreaming, and struggling, and looking forward to a new chapter in my life. Help me face the things that frighten me and rejoice in the life you have given me. Help me understand my dreams and myself. Amen.

✦ What have your dreams been like lately? What can they tell you about yourself? Can you relate to Jacob struggling through the night with a stranger?

"How beautiful you are, my love, how very beautiful! Your eyes are like doves behind your veil. Your hair is like a flock of goats, moving down the slopes of Gilead . . . Your neck is like the tower of David, built in courses; on it hang a thousand bucklers, all of them shields of warriors."
—Song of Solomon 4:1,4

"How beautiful you are, my love, how very beautiful!" It helps to hear someone say something like this to you once in a while. We all want to be beautiful, at least to those who know and love us. Few of us ever achieve the fashion-model kind of beauty we see in most ads. Still, every woman can glow with her own special beauty.

This is never more true than when you are pregnant. Otherwise ordinary features can sparkle with the joy of participating in a miracle. Bags under the eyes or troubles with your complexion pale in the glow of walking around with a miracle inside! Wear your blossoming belly as a badge of honor; carry yourself in a noble posture. Your bulging abdomen is a sign of blessing for all of us.

Maybe you're not so sure that pregnancy is an advantage in terms of beauty. Maybe you're beginning to feel like a blimp. Maybe the man in your life seems put off by your new figure. If so, now is the time to expand your vision of beauty. Twiggy women haven't always been the ideal of beauty. Check out a few art history books from the library; then look up the seventeenth-century painter Peter Paul Rubens. He painted beautiful, plump, sensuous women. These women smack of fruitfulness and plenty. Then think of all the beautiful round shapes you can—the golden curves of a juicy ripe pear, the firm purple oval of a luscious plum, the fluffy white billows of a beautiful cloud, the soft curves of a madonna's bosom, the golden halo that artists paint around the heads of the holy. Your rounding shape is fruitful and beautiful and holy, too.

To expand your vision of beauty still more, take another look at the snippet of love poetry that begins this meditation. Imagine describing a woman's beauty the way Solomon does: Your hair is like a flock of goats! Your neck is like a fort! Do these sound like compliments? Probably not to you and me, but for Solomon they must have described the rich abundance of his beloved's long wavy hair and the nobility and strength of her jewel encircled throat. Solomon also describes her teeth as like a flock of fertile, freshly washed and shorn sheep, all of which bear healthy twins! Beauty is in the eye of the beholder, as someone once said.

So when you look in the mirror, look for your beauty. Train your eye to see the beauty in your own body and soul, and in the body and soul of those around you. You are beautiful—so take good care of yourself. Get as much rest as you can. Payattention to your hair and makeup. Put on something pretty. Beauty is much more than surface prettiness, of course. Remember to show forth the beauty of your soul, too. Put on a cheerful expression to go with those pretty clothes. Share your joy and wisdom. Reach out with your love and kindness. Clothe your words and deeds with dignity and grace. In short, let your beautiful spirit and your holy work shine through all your features. "How beautiful you are, my love. How very beautiful!"

Dear God, you know that I don't always feel beautiful. Forgive me for finding this or that fault with the body you have given me. Help me to love myself in a healthy way. Help me see the beautiful person you created me to be. Help me let that beauty show forth in all that I say and do. In Jesus' name, Amen.

✦ What makes a person beautiful? Has pregnancy expanded your sense of beauty?

***"Wonderful are your works; that I know very well.
My frame was not hidden from you, when I was being
made in secret, intricately woven in the depths of the earth.
Your eyes beheld my unformed substance. In your book
were written all the days that were formed for me,
when none of them as yet existed."
—Psalm 139:14-16***

Have you taken a ride on the pregnancy roller coaster yet? One moment you almost burst with happiness at being so intensely alive. Then zoom—the whole world seems to slip away from under you. You feel like bursting into tears because someone looks at you the wrong way. Maybe you do burst into tears.

Many of us have moody days even when we're not pregnant. Pregnancy, though, seems to make our moods swing more than usual. Maybe it's the hormones. Maybe it's all the adjustments you're making. Maybe pregnancy is simply so primal an experience that it shakes you up and focuses your attention on life in all its raw splendor and terror.

The ups and downs and unexpected swings of pregnancy's emotional roller coaster may be more than you had bargained for. Some women shock themselves with their unusually powerful emotions and changeability. They fear they are losing their grip. Don't worry if you feel this way. You are not alone. Many pregnant women experience these mood swings. Just ask around among your pregnant or recently pregnant friends. Their stories may well be wilder than your own. Sharing stories can help you take your mood swings in stride. Who knows, you may even begin to see some humor in the craziness. After all, what's a roller-coaster ride without company? Talk to your husband about your mood swings, too. He will probably be able to take the ups and downs better if he knows that they often accompany pregnancy and that they usually even out again once you all get into the swing of life with a baby.

Remember, too, that your extra sensitivity reflects the tremendous spiritual activity going on within you during these months of change and growth. Welcome this extra sensitivity. It will pass quickly enough again. In a way, you are like a poet: you see many of the same things you saw before you were pregnant, but you see them in a completely new way. Things you might not even have noticed a few months ago now seem utterly precious. Things that wouldn't have phased you then now strike you as dangerous or heartless. Birds may warble more beautifully than ever before. Chubby toddler fingers exploring a wrinkled elderly cheek may pull at your heartstrings like never before. A carelessly trampled flower may seem more significant than ever before.

Record these impressions in your journal. Explore them, play with them, and search for the meanings they hold. Share your thoughts with a friend or someone you think of as a spiritual guide. It takes courage to explore the mysteries of your own spirit and the mysteries of life that touch you so deeply at this time, so remember that God is in this with you. God has known you ever since you were the little one being woven in secret. God made a journal entry describing your days way before those days even existed. God takes an interest in you, knows you, and loves you. God will help you understand your wildest emotions and your greatest challenges. God will help you see and play your part in the grand scheme of things.

Enjoy the roller-coaster ride with all its thrills and chills. Remember, God knows how you're put together. God knows how much excitement you can take. So be of good cheer—for, as the psalmist says, wonderful are God's works; that we know very well!

Dear Jesus, you know what it's like to have all kinds of emotions. Help me learn to live with mine. And you know all about the wonders and terrors of life. Keep me from taking the wonders for granted, and help me feel you standing by my side when I face the terrors. Help me enjoy the roller-coaster ride, confident in your power and love. Thank you for being there. Amen.

✦ What are the funniest, saddest, strangest, and most beautiful moments you have experienced recently?

"Do not neglect to show hospitality to strangers, for by doing that some have entertained angels without knowing it."
—Hebrews 13:2

"I got back the results of my amniocentesis, Pastor." Lisa was about forty, and expecting her first child. "My doctor advises 'old ladies' like me to have it—there's a higher risk of bearing a mongoloid baby when you're my age. It turned out all right," she hurried on, seeing my concerned look. "But I felt a little like a traitor even having it done. I mean, there's not much point in having the test if you're not willing to act on the results. But could we have coped with a handicapped child? I just don't know. Anyway, we don't have to worry about that now."

How do you respond to the offer of tests that can give you a sneak preview of your unborn child? Some women jump at the chance to see an ultrasound image of the guest hidden in their womb. Especially during early pregnancy, seeing even a hazy picture of a budding baby or hearing its heartbeat over scratchy background noise can assure you that someone really is in there. Other women prefer not to bombard their child with unnecessary ultrasound waves. Some women feel most secure when they have undergone every available screening. Other women prefer not to risk the worry and turmoil caused by inconclusive or misleading test results.

The availability of such tests presents you with moral questions never faced by your grandmother. She never had the option of weighing the good of seeing and tracking her baby by ultrasound against the uncharted possibility of damage inflicted by too much testing. She never had to consider what she would do if amniocentesis results predicted that her baby would probably be born with severe health problems.

Where do you stand? Maybe you make the decision easily, because you know that you would not interfere with your unborn baby no matter what test results showed. Maybe you find yourself at the other end of the spectrum: you may feel so unable to cope with a handicapped child that you know already that you would terminate the pregnancy if the results came out bad. Then again you may feel like Lisa: you take the test for the sense of security it promises to provide and pray hard that the results won't force you to make a decision you would rather avoid.

Pray about your decisions, just as you pray for your baby's

health. Under current law, no one can force you either to undergo amniocentesis or to carry an unwanted baby to term. Still, you need not bear the burden of such life-and-death questions alone. Talk to your husband, a respected friend, your pastor. The wisdom and support available to you through the community of faith can give you the insight and courage to make the best possible decision for you and your child.

As you pray, remember that even if your test results are good, you can't expect a perfect child. Some will turn out to have poor eyesight; others will have teeth that grow in crooked. Some will have trouble coordinating their muscles; others will have trouble controlling their tempers. We all have our weaknesses, and our children will have theirs, too. Children who have disabilities are not in a class by themselves. They are human beings like all the rest of us, with their own particular combination of strengths and weaknesses, gifts and troubles.

Still, a handicapped child does call for extra care. A child with special needs may introduce a level of stress that can fray family ties. On the other hand, I know from experience that with God's help the presence of such a child can draw a family together. My younger sister Sonja was born with health problems that meant much extra work for my mother and many trips to the hospital, but Sonja brought countless blessings to our entire family.

Sonja was an angel. That is not to say that she was always sweet; she had her bad days, too. Still she was an angel—an angel who taught us to appreciate life, whatever our limitations. I think of her when I read the book of Hebrews' call to extend hospitality to strangers—strangers who may turn out to be angels. Some strangers we can see and size up when they knock on our door. Others enter our lives from within. Even now you are extending the hospitality of your womb to a little stranger. Perhaps this little stranger will turn out to be a child so brilliant that you wonder how to best nurture her. Perhaps he will be a child with a body so weak that it can scarcely contain his radiantly loving soul. Perhaps he or she will have some completely different combination of strengths and weaknesses. Who knows, the little stranger nestled in your womb may turn out to be an angel bearing unexpected blessings!

Dear God, thank you for giving me knowledge and the ability to choose. Thank you for giving me people that I can talk things over with. Help me make good decisions for my baby and me. Give us both good health, and give us strength to live with our weaknesses. Help me live one day at a time, confident that you will be with me through all of life's challenges. Amen.

✦ Have you undergone prenatal screening? Why or why not?

"When the [stranger with whom Jacob had struggled through the night] saw that he did not prevail against Jacob, he struck him on the hip socket; and Jacob's hip was put out of joint as he wrestled with him. Then he said, 'Let me go, for the day is breaking.' But Jacob said, 'I will not let you go, unless you bless me.' . . . Then the man said, 'You shall no longer be called Jacob, but Israel, for you have striven with God and with humans and you have prevailed.'"
—Genesis 32:25 f., 28

I try to take a walk every day. Usually I leave the house with brisk, purposeful strides. My walking partner, our little dog Pilli, looks forward to her walk with such energy that she strains at the leash and pulls me ahead. No dallying, no swerving: onward! So we charge ahead until Pilli's urge to make tracks gives way to her urge to sniff things out.

Pilli and I see many walking styles on our tours through the neighborhood. Mothers push strollers slowly to match their toddlers' pace. Flocks of teenagers move a few steps, stop for a bit while they joke and tease, then amble on again. Power walkers zoom along, trim in their lycra outfits. Colorful pairs of older women, draped in saris and scarves from head to foot, sway back and forth as they make their way ponderously down the street.

Where do you fit in? Do you hike easily and quickly along when you go out for your exercise? Or has your body's new shape begun to slow you down? Maybe you have begun to waddle a little. As pregnancy progresses, ligaments soften and joints loosen in preparation for birth. Even something as simple as walking becomes a new experience.

How do you feel about your changing body? I knew a young woman who was so proud to be pregnant that she stuck out her stomach almost before there was anything to stick out. She beamed as she strutted around showing off her condition. Another woman held her tummy in as long as possible. She took pride in *not* showing. Such different reactions to the body's changes—and yet both women were happy to be pregnant.

Maybe you enjoy letting your body do its own thing. For once you feel good when you discover that you can't button your jeans! On the other hand, your rapidly changing figure may distress you. You may resent your bulging tummy, especially if you weren't planning to get pregnant. Even if you wanted to get pregnant, you may find it unnerving to watch your body take charge and make such dramatic changes. You may be proud of your bulging belly, or embarrassed by it. You may feel both ways—proud of your fertility, but a little embarrassed by such clear evidence of your sex life.

Don't worry if you have conflicting feelings. They reflect the important part our bodies play in our self-image. Think of those teenagers ambling down the street: their bubbling hormones put them through all kinds of hoops, trying to figure out who they are in their changing bodies. Adolescence brings on plenty of identity-challenging changes—but those changes emerge very gradually compared to the fast pace of change during pregnancy. No wonder you have mixed feelings!

Some days you may feel like a duck waddling around. Other days you may feel like a full-sailed ship moving majestically and purposefully ahead. Some days you may even catch a glimpse of yourself in the mirror and wonder, "Is that really me?"

Explore your feelings and the images that come to your mind. Your new body shape may teach you unexpected lessons. You feel like Jemima Puddleduck? Your pregnant body can give you insight into our kinship with all God's creatures. You feel like a sailing ship? Your roomy body can remind you of the elegance of God's creation.

However you feel, ask God to help you take the changing shape of your body into your sense of self. Love your changing body; wonder at it; learn to have patience with it. There may be days when you find it hard to accept your body's new shape and the changes it brings into your life. That's all right. Ask God to help you grow through all your feelings, the bad as well as the good.

Think of Jacob wrestling through the night with an unknown opponent. He didn't run away or give up, and he finally prevailed. He went on his way with a limp, but also with a noble new identity. He received a new name, "Israel," the one who strives with God. Jacob didn't know it at the time, but he had struggled with God. So, too, when you struggle to take your changing body into yourself, you struggle with God. God created you with capabilities and limitations: Your body is already showing its stretching capabilities, while your will is running up against its limited power to call all the shots. In the midst of these changes, God holds on to you while you test your confidence, flexibility, and willingness to let nature take its course.

This struggle will both mark you and bless you. Most of the changes of pregnancy are not permanent: You won't waddle forever. Still, some marks remain. Stretch marks will fade, but they never disappear completely. So, too, the stretch marks on your soul will stay with you. You will always know that your body did magnificent things: it stretched and embraced, it nourished and protected. Your body's silvery stretch marks will remind you that your spirit, too, stretched and struggled and was eventually blessed with a noble new identity: mother.

Dear God, thank you for making me a body that can do such wonderful things! Help me to rejoice in my body and take good care of it. Help me take my body's changes in stride. Give me patience when my body slows me down. Give me courage to face feelings that scare me. Give me eyes to see the changes as a sign of your grace and goodness. Help me grow in spirit even as my baby grows within me. Amen.

✦ How have your body's changes affected your self-image?

"As many of you as were baptized into Christ have clothed yourselves with Christ. . . . Jesus Christ is the same yesterday and today and forever."
—Galatians 3:27 and Hebrews 13:8

Finding maternity clothes can be such fun. All of a sudden you really do *need* something new to wear! Maybe you've already received some roomy blouses or dresses from formerly pregnant friends. Maybe you've tried on things at the "becoming mother" store in the mall or the maternity clothes bank at your church. Maybe you've bought yard upon yard of fabric and have begun sewing a new wardrobe.

The great thing about trying on maternity clothes is that you don't have to worry too much about them fitting. They almost all fit—loosely speaking. Most of them are cut so loose, in fact, that when you try them on early in your pregnancy you may find it hard to imagine that you'll ever need *that* much room! If you usually wear loose-fitting clothes, you may not even need maternity clothes for several months. On the other hand, if you usually wear clothes with a tailored and close-fitting look, you may need roomier outfits early on, while you still find it hard to see yourself wearing clothes so huge.

In any case, take time to find clothes that you will enjoy wearing. When you start wearing those billowing dresses and funny stretch-topped pants, your pregnancy starts feeling more real. When you start wearing your new wardrobe, the world around you will also start to see you as an expecting mother. Do what you can to choose items that will make you feel and look your best as you start this new chapter in your life.

Like it or not, your new clothes will seem too big at first—you need room to grow. In this respect maternity clothes resemble baptismal gowns. Think of the long white gowns infants have traditionally worn at their baptism. Families often hand them down from sibling to sibling and from one generation to the next. They fit both a scrawny little infant and a plumper, more robust one. Any baby has plenty of room for thick diapers and plenty of kicking under the ample folds of cloth. So, too, the white robes sometimes worn by adults being baptized are roomy, one-size-fits-all garments, like the white robes worn by many worship leaders.

Maternity clothes, with their room to grow, resemble even more the spiritual garment we all put on at our baptism. Saint Paul reminds us that when we were baptized we clothed ourselves in Christ. Imagine that spiritual garment—pure and radiantly beautiful, flowing and large enough for any of us to spend a lifetime growing into. This lovely garment is not immediately visible, of course, but it can be glimpsed through eyes open to the spirit. Seen through such eyes, the spiritual garment you put on at your baptism tells something important about you. Just as your maternity clothes show the world that you're on your way to becoming a new mother, this lovely spiritual garment shows that you belong to Christ and are growing into your Christian identity every day.

Many things are changing in your life right now. Your body is changing so much that you need a whole new set of clothes. Your appetite is changing. Your sex life may be changing. Your self-image will be stretching and changing to include a picture of you mothering your new child. Your thoughts and feelings and priorities have probably been spinning as you think ahead to the new roles and responsibilities that await you. You may be considering changes in your work life, or changes in your housing arrangements to make space for the newcomer.

In the midst of all of these changes, remember that some things never change. Christ is the same yesterday and today and forever. That lovely spiritual garment you put on at your baptism will continue to clothe and shield you no matter how much your body changes. That roomy spiritual dress proclaims a lasting identity that no amount of role changes or awesome new responsibilities can take from you. You have put on Christ, and the Holy Spirit will help you rise to all life's challenges. The Spirit will help you grow day by day in Christ's lovely newness of life.

Dear Jesus, thank you for staying with me through all of life's changes. Give me your peace as I learn to live with all the changes facing me. Help me enjoy every moment of life—the changes, the waiting, the challenges, the pleasures. Teach me to love as you loved. Help me to grow more and more like you in grace and holiness. Amen

✦ How do you feel about the changes in your life? How do you think motherhood might affect your growth as a Christian?

4

New Relationships

"When [Zechariah] did come out, he could not speak to them, and they realized that he had seen a vision in the sanctuary. He kept motioning to them and remained unable to speak."
—Luke 1:22

The Walt Disney story *Lady and the Tramp* tells what happens to a nice little dog named Lady when her humans, Darling and Jim Dear, have a baby. Even before the baby arrives, Lady notices a difference in Jim Dear and Darling. Jim Dear doesn't run and play with her like he used to, and Darling spends her time sitting, knitting, and gazing out into thin air.

Maybe you, too, find yourself gazing dreamily out into thin air more often than usual. Your husband, too, may have changed some. Perhaps he opens more doors and carries more packages for you or shows extra concern about what you eat and how you feel. On the other hand, he may seem unusually withdrawn. If so, you probably wonder what's going on inside his head: Does he want this child? Is he worried about the extra responsibility? Is he just trying to figure out how to act in this new situation?

A new child in the family does turn the world upside down for a while, as Lady found out. Pregnancy gives you and your mate time to prepare yourselves to meet the challenges of the upcoming wild and wonderful days. You need those hours of daydreaming. He needs time to sort things out, too.

Sometimes, though, you may feel very alone with your pregnancy and all that it will mean in your life. Maybe you wonder how much your husband will help you, and you don't dare ask him. Maybe you wish your parents would mother you more—or that they would smother you less—and you don't know how to tell them.

Like John the Baptist's father, Zechariah, you may feel locked in silence. Zechariah couldn't believe it when the angel told him that he and his elderly wife Elizabeth would soon become parents—so the angel silenced Zechariah as a sign that the prophecy was true. Although your mouth and vocal cords still work as usual, and your family and friends know that you are expecting, you may feel unable to talk freely about the changes going on inside you. Perhaps you sometimes feel like Zechariah, wrestling silently with the angel's blessing and your response to it. Unspoken doubts or regrets push their way into your thoughts and demand your attention. You struggle to hold on to your joy and wonder at the miracle unfolding within you.

Your husband can probably also relate to Zechariah. He faces big changes in his life, too—changes that he cannot grasp all at once. Perhaps he finds it hard to put his feelings into words; many men learn to hide their emotions rather than express them. Perhaps he feels especially protective of you at this time and is trying to shield you from his concerns. Perhaps he simply needs time for the reality of your pregnancy to sink in. He doesn't experience the effects of pregnancy in his own body as you do; he may barely notice them at first. You can focus on your physical sensations and try to distinguish the baby's first unmistakable leap; he must wait until the baby is big enough for its movements to be felt through your abdominal wall. It may all seem unreal to him at first.

Learn to read your silence as a sign—a sign that your pregnancy is a spiritual occasion for both you and your husband, a sign that God continues to bless us even when we cannot quite see or believe it. Spiritual growth begins in these silent struggles to understand and respond to the blessings and challenges God sends us. So don't be too hard on yourselves when you or your mate seems locked in silence. Remember that Zechariah the priest was no spiritual slouch. Indeed, the Bible makes a point of telling us that both he and his wife were righteous and blameless people. Still, even Zechariah couldn't immediately accept the angel's promise, so he spent months wrestling with it in silence. Remember, too, that Zechariah eventually emerged from his silence. And when he did, he came out praising God and overflowing with the Spirit!

Note also that Elizabeth and Zechariah must have found some way to communicate, in spite of Zechariah's silenced vocal cords. By the time their baby was born, Elizabeth knew that the angel had instructed Zechariah to name their baby John. Respect one another's need for peace and quiet to work things through in your own minds, but also find ways to share your hopes and fears at this crossroads in your life. Pray for each other, pray together if you can. Do all you can to strengthen your relationship now so you will be in better shape to weather the challenges ahead.

O God, thank you for giving us one another. Thank you for the baby growing inside me. Thank you for the people who love me. Guide me when I struggle silently to make sense of myself and my life. Give me the courage and wisdom and words to open up to those who care about me. Help me strengthen my personal relationships, for my baby's sake as well as for my own. Amen.

✦ Do you have concerns that you are reluctant to discuss? What holds you back? How has your husband reacted to your pregnancy?

"I would lead you and bring you into the house of my mother, and into the chamber of the one who bore me."
—Song of Solomon 8:2

"Can a woman forget her nursing child, or show no compassion for the child of her womb? Even these may forget, yet I will not forget you."
—Isaiah 49:15

"How does it feel to be a mom?" our seven-year old asked as she snuggled in under the covers with me.

"Usually it feels pretty good—especially when your little girl comes in and cuddles and chats for a while before it's time to get up," I answered.

What will it feel like to be a mom? Or, if you already have children: What will it feel like to be the mother of another child? You probably have been asking yourself such questions since you found out that you are pregnant. Maybe you have been asking your own mother, too: How did it feel to become a mother? How did you manage?

Even if you haven't asked your mother these questions directly, you probably find yourself thinking about her more than you usually do. You may think about how she raised you—mulling over things you hope to do as well as she did, and things you hope to do differently in bringing up your own children. Old wounds and needs may rise to the surface: Some women wish that their mothers would mother them and appreciate them more; others wish their mothers would back off and let them try their own wings. At the same time, you may feel a new sense of intimacy and sisterhood with your mother. You may gain new respect for her as you start thinking about childhood from a mother's perspective.

The Bible doesn't say much specifically about the relationship of daughters to their mothers, but Solomon indirectly suggests that lovemaking and birthgiving are points in a daughter's life when she naturally revisits her mother. The woman in his love poetry longs to draw her lover into her mother's chamber. A few verses later he sings of having awakened her under the apple tree where her mother gave birth to her. Everything seems to come together in the mother's chamber. The circle of life is completed and carried on. The lovers are knit together—with each other, with the generations before them, and with the generation to come.

So, too, your pregnancy invites you into your mother's chamber. It gives you a chance to see your life from her perspective. It gives you a chance to forgive her for her shortcomings and honor her for her gifts. It gives you a chance to acknowledge her style of mothering and then get on with shaping your own.

Take this opportunity to grow in your relationship to your mother. If you are able, share your joys and fears, and listen to hers. Ask about the story of your own birth. Many of us grow to adulthood knowing little about the circumstances of our birth. Your pregnancy provides a natural occasion to learn more about your own beginnings and to see your mother as a sister facing challenges like those you face now.

Perhaps you cannot ask about your own birth. Your mother may have died or have no contact with you. The mother who gave you birth may have given you up for adoption; the mother who raised you may know very little about the circumstances of your conception and birth. Your own pregnancy may bring unanswered questions and sorrows to the surface again. If this is the case, ask God to help you accept the things you cannot change and to heal whatever wounds you bear upon your soul.

Perhaps you can talk to your mother but have difficulty doing so. If your relationship needs mending, pray about it. Then speak as honestly and lovingly as you can about what troubles you. Tell your mother that you need space if she seems overbearing.

Ask her for help if you need and want it. Pray for forgiveness and healing.

We all need plenty of grace and forgiveness as we take on the responsibility of mothering. We mother to the best of our abilities, but even the best mother has blind spots and failings. As the prophet Isaiah tells us, even the powerful love of human mothers may fail—but the mother love of God will never fail. This strong, mothering God will remember you and help you grow in your relationship to your mother. This strong, mothering God will help you mother your own children.

We all model ourselves initially after our mothers: My little girl looks first to me when she starts figuring out what mothering means. Yet none of us is locked in her mother's chamber. Every generation remodels more or less extensively the model of mothering they received: We express our own personalities. We share our lives with new people and the traditions and models of parenting they bring. We live in a world that changes from one generation to the next. With God's help you will pass on the healthy and good things you learned in your mother's chamber, forgive her for her failings, and forgive yourself for your own.

Dear God, thank you for my family, for all they did to raise me and for all they mean to me today. Help me grow in my relationship to my mother. Help us learn to love and respect one other as adults. Help me learn to be a good mother myself. Give me wisdom and humor, strengthen me with the confidence that you will remember me and help me. Amen.

✦ How do you think your style of mothering will resemble your mother's style? How will it differ?

"Therefore a man leaves his father and his mother and clings to his wife, and they become one flesh."
—Genesis 2:24

"Leah conceived and bore a son, and she named him Reuben; for she said, 'Because the Lord has looked on my affliction; surely now my husband will love me.'"
—Genesis 29:32

In the middle of my first pregnancy, a friend told me that he had not felt really married until he and his wife started having children. His comment startled me at the time: my husband and I had tied the knot several years earlier, and I felt plenty married. "Before we had kids," he said, "our relationship wasn't much different than it was when we were going out together. Okay, so we became roommates. Big deal. We didn't have to rearrange our lives much. But when our son was born, things changed. All of a sudden we had responsibility for someone other than ourselves. We couldn't just go see a movie on the spur of the moment like we could before. Judy and I became a team in a way we hadn't needed to before."

Having a baby together can make you and the baby's father more of a team. I think that's part of what the Bible means when it says a husband and wife become one flesh. The child growing in your womb is a bit of your union fleshed out into a unique new person. From now on, your genes and those of your man will intertwine in the flesh of your child. No matter what the future brings, this child of your union gives the two of you something special in common. For most couples, a shared child gives extra incentive to stick together. Perhaps that is why a pregnancy often leads couples who have lived together for years to get married.

The responsibilities and joys of parenthood can bring couples closer together. You work together to ready a space for your baby. Your husband holds your hand during childbirth. You beam at one another when your child takes her first step and says his first word. Together you rearrange priorities and schedules; your partnership takes on a new purpose and new pleasures.

It doesn't automatically work out that way though. Leah bore child after child, hoping that in doing so she would win her husband's love. It never seemed to work. Babies are wonderful, but they aren't glue. They won't magically patch together shaky relationships. The demands a baby makes on parents may even drive a wedge between the two of them. Don't let this happen to you if you can help it!

Make a special effort to nurture your relationship with your husband at this special time in your lives. You both face new challenges; make a point of talking things out. Your husband may wonder how you will be able to afford this child and if he'll make a good father. He may feel extra protective of you and wonder if having sex will hurt the baby. He may feel left out and overlooked, and then ashamed of himself for feeling jealous of his own unborn baby. Make the effort to listen—and to tell about your hopes and fears, too. What better time to practice listening and caring for one another!

Your shared pregnancy is a good time for the two of you to grow closer, but don't feel that you must serve as each other's sole confidant. Your husband may benefit from some man-to-man talk about pregnancy and fatherhood, just as some woman-to-woman talk can give you a boost and some practical tips. If your friends can't relate to the thrills and chills of pregnancy, look for an expecting parents' support group. Your church may offer pre-birth baptismal or parenting classes; if not, ask about starting one. Community-sponsored childbirth preparation classes, too, can lead to friendships and moral support.

Finally, remember that there's more to becoming one flesh than making babies together. Your love for your husband began before your baby. With God's help, and commitment from you and your spouse, your love will continue long after your youngest child grows up and flies from the nest. Imagine all the ways you might express your love over the course of a lifetime. An unexpected kindness here, a word of apology or forgiveness there—little things go a long way. At this very moment you express your love for your mate by the very bodily business of bearing his child within you.

Take pregnancy as an occasion to expand and explore your lovemaking. If you often feel nauseated, you may prefer gentle stroking and cuddling to full-fledged intercourse. But feel free to have sex if you like; it won't hurt your baby. He or she is safely cushioned by the waters of your womb, and a mucous plug seals the opening of the womb until it's time for you to give birth. You may well enjoy finding ways to get around your ripening belly! In any case, use your bodies, as well as your words and deeds, as ways to express the love that you have been given to share.

Dear God, thank you for giving us each other to love, and for giving us so many ways to express our love. Help us learn to love each other better each day. Help us stand by each other and face the changes of life with grace and humor. Amen.

✦ How do you think pregnancy and a new child will affect your relationship with your mate? How do you plan to continue building that relationship as your family grows?

"The angel of the Lord said to [Hagar], 'Return to your mistress, and submit to her.' The angel of the Lord also said to her, 'I will so greatly multiply your offspring that they cannot be counted for multitude.'"
—Genesis 16:9-10

"That's it," Veronica said as she clicked off the television set. "If I hear one more word about perverts abusing children or babies born with AIDS, I'm going to go nuts." She sat down and cried. "What kind of world are we bringing our little one into?"

Some wellness experts will tell you that watching the evening news can be hazardous to your health. All that bad news can give you a warped picture of the world. You end up depressed and less vigorous than you were before.

We do live in a troubled world (although it's not as bad as one would think based solely on news reports). Rearing children in this world will take all the courage and wisdom you can muster. You're not alone in facing this important task, though. No matter how troubled the world, no matter how chaotic your own personal circumstances, God promises to stay with you and help you.

On days when you think you've got your troubles, remember Hagar. (You can read about her for yourself in Genesis 16:1-11 and 21:9-21.) Hagar was a slave girl who may well be the world's first recorded case of a surrogate mother. Her mistress, Abram's wife, Sarai, was so desperate for a child that she sent Hagar in to Abram as her proxy. The plan seemed to work: Hagar got pregnant. This did not solve Sarai's problems, though. Hagar was a human being with feelings, not just a baby-making machine. She got a little uppity when she succeeded where her mistress had failed. Finally Sarai couldn't take it anymore. She told Abram her troubles, and he said, "Well she's your slave, do whatever you want with her." So Sarai let all her resentment and anger loose on Hagar, until Hagar ran away into the desert.

What a predicament: pregnant runaway slave, alone in the desert. How could she survive? Things looked bleak for Hagar, until at this very low point God came to her, counselled her, and blessed her. Hagar didn't have to earn God's help. The Bible doesn't even mention her praying. She was an Egyptian, so she might not have looked to Abram and Sarai's God for help. Still, God saw her in her troubles and came to her aid.

The story doesn't have a fairy-tale ending, though. God didn't send in Prince Charming to marry Hagar and whisk her away to become a royal princess. Instead, God helped Hagar see herself. People may have treated Hagar like a piece of property or a nameless baby-making machine, but God's angel treated her with respect and addressed her by name. The angel helped Hagar see that God valued her. Then the angel asked her where she came from and where she was going. In so doing, the angel helped Hagar look at the relationships she had run away from and at her prospects for the future. God helped Hagar look at her options and then told Hagar to choose life under a difficult mistress rather than death in the desert. Moreover, God gave Hagar a promise that would help her through the hard times ahead. God promised that Hagar's child would give her descendants too numerous to count.

Hagar returned to her old life and its problems—but as a new person. She returned with new self-respect and hope, and a new relationship to God. She returned to her tangled web of relationships strengthened by God's promise that her child would survive and thrive. We don't know if Hagar lived happily ever after. We don't know how well she got along with Sarai. The Bible does tell us that fourteen years later Sarai's jealousy finally forced Hagar and her son, Ishmael, out into the desert for good. It also tells us that Ishmael did become the father of a great nation.

Fortunately, few of us find ourselves in such difficult circumstances. Even if you do have rocky family relationships or financial troubles, you live in a society where help is available. Seek out the help you need, for your baby's sake and your own. Government programs offer financial assistance to those in need. Churches, women's counselling services, family, and friends can help you deal with troubled relationships.

Few of us find ourselves in Hagar's precarious predicament, but we all need help raising our children in a troubled world. Even if you are blessed with a relatively healthy marriage and financial stability, you may have days when you wonder how you will manage. Take this occasion to strengthen your relationships. As time goes on, you and your child will benefit from the love, wisdom, and support of family, friends, and church community. None of these relationships are perfect. Still, God works through them to help and guide you. Like Hagar, take stock of your situation. Which relationships nourish you most; which need extra attention? Which way are you headed; are you on the right track? Count the ways God cares for you. Ask the Spirit to help you bring healing and hope to relationships that trouble you. God gave Hagar the courage and wisdom to make the best of her situation. God will help you, too.

Dear God, thank you for standing by me through thick and thin. Help me make wise choices and give my baby a good start on life. Lift me up when I am down, and give me the courage to face life's troubles. Help me bring a touch of health and happiness to the world around me. Amen.

✦ What is the greatest challenge facing you as you begin raising a family? Who may be able to help you rise to the challenge?

"A capable wife who can find?
She is far more precious than jewels."
—Proverbs 31:10

To work or not to work—that is the question. Or is it? All mothers work, even if they don't all get a paycheck. If you have been working outside the home, you may be deciding whether or not to keep your job after your baby arrives. One woman I know had no trouble making the decision: "I know I'd crawl the walls if I didn't get out of the house at least a few hours a day." Another would have loved to stay home while her children were young but didn't see how her family could manage on her husband's salary alone. A third decided to risk leaving the paid work force for a few years and planned to scale down and budget carefully to make ends meet.

I don't know any easy answers. Juggling work schedules, child-care arrangements, time for yourself, and time with your mate can leave you feeling like the ringmaster in a three-ring circus. On the other hand, opting out of the work force means a radical change in your life. You may miss contact with coworkers as well as the paycheck. You may miss the respect gainful employment often brings, even though you might enjoy the newfound opportunity to organize your own day.

Working out a good balance may not be easy, but it is possible. Throughout the ages, women have managed to juggle marketable work with household responsibilities, relationships, and community service. If you have any doubt about that, read the description of a capable wife in Proverbs 31. This woman seeks out raw materials and transforms them into food and clothing. She manages servants. She invests in real estate and produces profitable merchandise. She helps the poor and worships the

Lord, and she speaks with wisdom and kindness. Her community respects her, and her family loves her. What more can any of us hope to accomplish?

Let this capable foremother inspire you as you think through your own priorities, gifts, and needs. Jot down the many tasks that you do at home and on the job. You may surprise yourself with the long list you come up with! List the new responsibilities you can foresee coming with the birth of your child, both in terms of time and of finances. Which things are most important? Which do you do best and enjoy most? Which tasks could you share with your spouse or older children? If keeping your job is high on your list of priorities, look into your employer's maternity-leave policy and explore your scheduling and child-care options. If you plan to quit your job, start looking for new sources of friendship and camaraderie.

Pray through your lists and plans and questions. Ask God to help you know yourself—your abilities and your limitations, your values and your joys. The better you know yourself, the better you will be able to find a balance that suits you. Talk things through carefully with your husband and pray with him, too. Ask God to help the two of you set healthy priorities for yourselves and your family. Plan together how you can best share the new responsibilities and joys that are coming your way. Remember to factor in some wiggle room, too. You will need breathing space for yourself; you will need time to spend together as a couple; you will need time for church and community as time to put daily bread on the table.

Thinking and praying carefully about your decision will give you confidence to rise to the challenges that lie ahead. If you decide to stay home with your children, prayerful forethought will help you do so with pride. Staying home doesn't whittle you down to "just a housewife." You are a person who has chosen to focus her talents on homemaking and mothering. If you decide to keep your job, prayerful forethought will help you avoid the "superwoman" trap. Discuss how you will share household duties—and then let go of the responsibilities your spouse agrees to take. If you don't have the support of a spouse, prayerful forethought will help you take each day in stride. You may not have a husband to help you, but God will help you find ways to bear your burdens.

Finally, remember that you have a whole lifetime to become all God hopes for you. You don't have to do everything all at once. Take this chance to figure out what is most important to you as a person and your family at this time. Then go ahead, doing first things first. The first few months after your child's birth will probably feel chaotic no matter what you decide. Don't lose heart: you will live through the topsy-turvy days and nights. What's more, those topsy-turvy days and nights can shake any of us into doing first things first—feeding and calming a hungry child goes right to the top of the list, dirty laundry gets unceremoniously bumped.

Shaking up assumptions and sorting through priorities is a healthy spiritual exercise. You might say that it makes the difference between a person who is like a diamond in the rough and one who is like a sparkling gem. A sparkling gem catches the light and reflects it in beautiful new ways because the lesser material has been carefully trimmed away, and the surface has been cut and polished into many complementary facets. Use this new chapter in your life as a time to take stock, a time to trim away the less important items from your schedule, a time to uncover new facets in yourself.

Dear God, help me to see myself as you see me. Thank you for giving me talents and options, and help me face my limitations. Guide my decisions, and help me balance the new joys and cares coming into my life. Show me how to become the jewel of a person you created me to be. In Jesus' name, Amen.

✦ How do you think God is calling you to use your talents and skills at this time in your life?

"Her children rise up and call her happy; her husband too, and he praises her: 'Many women have done excellently, but you surpass them all.'"
—Proverbs 31:28 f.

After I found out I was pregnant with our first child, my husband and I started signing our letters: *Jørgen and Margaret (+)*. Soon we began referring to our unborn child as "Plus." "Plus" seemed like the perfect temporary name for this new person we were expecting. I hadn't even felt the baby's first kick when we started using that name. We didn't know if our baby would be a boy or a girl. All we knew was that we expected a plus in our lives.

You may already have given your unborn child a nickname of some sort, too. Somehow a name, even if it's only a temporary one, makes the unknown entity hidden in your womb more of a person. You can talk to someone with a name, even if you haven't seen him or her. Maybe you just call your baby "baby" or "little one." Whatever you call the fetus forming inside you, you are already beginning to form a relationship that will last a lifetime.

This relationship with an unseen partner mirrors our relationship to God. God and your baby may both be hidden for the time being, but you can see evidence of them both. Your swelling belly shows you that your baby is growing. Daily bread on the table, friendship, and experiences of grace are all signs of God's blessing. You can talk to our hidden God, just as you can talk to the child hidden in your womb. Moreover, sooner or later you will see both of them face to face. You will see and hold your baby within a few months, and, as the apostle Paul writes, "now we see in a mirror dimly, but then we shall see face to face" (1 Corinthians. 13:12).

Mirrors reflect an image that is identical, but opposite. The relationship between you and your unseen baby mirrors the relationship between you and our unseen God with one important difference. You know about your baby, care for it and nourish it and start talking to it before it can talk to you. With God it's the other way around—God has known you, cared for you, and reached out to you before you could even call out for help.

Your relationship with God will last a lifetime and grow with you. So, too, the relationship that you begin now with your child will grow and change over time. Soon you will be able to see your child. You'll choose a permanent name for him or her and register it in the public record. Soon conversations with your baby will no longer be one way monologues. You'll hear your child's voice—screaming for attention at some times, gurgling contentedly at others. A few months later you'll be deciphering your child's first attempts to say your name and holding out your hands to encourage baby's first unsteady steps. Before you know it, your child will be telling you the newest jokes and asking for help with homework.

Little by little, our children grow up and try their wings. We don't know in advance exactly what they will be like: Will they be serious or playful? Swaggering or shy? Will they be athletes or musicians? Scholars or entrepreneurs? Will things come easily for them, or will they have more than their share of struggles? I love watching the mysterious unfolding of our children's talents and personalities—even though their unfolding quirks and needs call for all the parental skill and wisdom Jørgen and I can muster!

Parents can influence and guide their offspring, but we can't determine their lives. We don't create them; we relate to them. We do our best to provide for them, to teach and guide them, to show them we love them. We hope that they will grow into strong, loving, God-fearing people. In the process, we grow, too. We learn to change diapers and blow on "owies." We learn to wonder again at tadpoles changing into frogs and dandelions becoming ripe for blowing. We learn how to set reasonable limits and how to listen, when to help and when to back off. We learn patience and humility and the joys of simple pleasures. We don't learn our lessons perfectly any more than our children learn theirs perfectly. If nothing else, parenthood teaches one the importance of forgiveness! Still, with God's help we will live and learn, give and forgive, bless and be blessed.

When all is said and done, we hope that our children will see us as a blessing in their lives. We hope that the relationship that begins with them completely dependent upon us will blossom into mature love and freely given respect and friendship. Sometimes we wonder how that will all work out, but we trust our hidden God to help us. We can do that because we know that the children who add so much to our lives are not ours alone. We have them on loan by the grace of God. We love and teach and enjoy them; but ultimately they belong to God, as indeed we ourselves do.

Dear God, thank you for helping me believe in you, even though I can't see you. Thank you for the child hidden in my womb. Help me love my children as flesh of my flesh and still respect them as individuals belonging to you. In Jesus' name, Amen.

✦ What hopes do you have for your children? What gifts do you have to share with them? Where do you see God in your childrearing?

5

Coworkers in a Miracle

"Now the man knew his wife Eve, and she conceived and bore Cain, saying, 'I have produced a man with the help of the Lord.'"
—Genesis 4:1

I love this Bible verse. It sums up the Bible's understanding of how birth works, all in one elegant sentence. Right now you're about half way through this sentence—past the conceiving and well into the bearing. This middle period of pregnancy can be delightful: the nausea of early pregnancy has diminished; your belly has begun to blossom, but it still doesn't cramp your style too much; your baby has made it safely through the critical first months. This time of peaceful growing offers a good opportunity to think about the creative work you are doing.

The Bible teaches that making babies is a creative partnership between you (and your mate) and God. Eve proclaims, "I have produced a man with the help of the Lord." You can hear the sense of satisfaction she feels from having produced a child from her own body. Just as important, she glories in working along with God to make such a miracle. She knows God has been with her, helping her all the way through the process.

Eve experienced giving birth as a spiritual event. Having a baby assured her that God was still active in her life. Imagine how important this assurance of God's presence was to Eve and her husband. It came when they were still adjusting to the harsh realities of life outside of Eden. Indeed, the verse that tells about the world's first birth comes right after the story of Adam and Eve leaving the Garden.

In its own understated way, this verse suggests a touching picture of Adam and Eve outside the Garden. You can almost see them huddling together in the wilderness. They think wistfully of the carefree life they have lost, and they weep at their own foolishness. They wonder if they have lost contact with God forever, and they comfort each other. Their embrace leads to "knowing" each other, as the Bible so graciously calls having sexual relations. A few months later the first baby ever is born. By that time Eve knows God in a new way, too. She knows that God's help reaches well beyond paradise. She and Adam can count on God all along the way.

Take time to think about how God has been working with you through this pregnancy. You may see God working through your family and friends to help you prepare for your baby. You may see God working through your midwife or doctor. You may feel specially blessed by the prayers of your church. You may feel incredibly blessed by the privilege of carrying a new life within you.

So, too, you may feel blessed to have such a wonderful, God-given body. Most of us focus more than usual on our bodies during pregnancy. Many of us learn amazing new things. I remember listening to a childbirth educator describe how womb muscles stretch this way and that to make room for a baby. Then, just when you'd think they'd be all stretched out, they contract until they push the baby out into the world. It's a miracle your womb can expand as it does; and it's a miracle those stretched womb muscles have the strength to contract so powerfully. The elastic waistbands on clothes I wore too long before shifting to maternity clothes sure never sprang back like that!

Cynics might argue that the details of human reproduction

are nothing new or particularly miraculous. You can read about them in any sex-education handbook. But does that argument do justice to the experience?

The writer of Genesis obviously knows how baby-making works. There is no mention of supernatural interventions, even to get the very first birth underway. This birth started just as births have for generations since—with good old-fashioned, down-to-earth sex: The man had sex with his wife; she got pregnant and gave birth. Right to the point, and very matter of fact, isn't it? No wonder people who were raised before sex was openly discussed often found the Bible a good place to learn the facts of life!

The writer of Genesis admits the facts of life right up front—and still sees birth as a miracle, a sign of God working with and through people. Getting pregnant and giving birth is very earthy business. Still, most of us sense that it is also a miracle. My internship congregation made this point very memorably at a going-away party they held for me. Most of them knew I was a few months pregnant, so they gave me two T-shirts. The first was huge. Printed boldly on the front was this caption: "The Miracle that happened at Prince of Peace." The second T-shirt was as tiny as they come. It sported a silver question mark and the caption "The Miracle"!

You, too, are working with God to make a miracle. Enjoy it! Glory in it! Let this down-to-earth, often-repeated miracle help you see God's hand in your life today and every day!

Dear God, thank you for giving me such a wonderful, creative body. Help me to see your hand in my life, and to trust that you will stand by me through thick and thin. Amen.

✦ What do you think is most wonderful about pregnancy and childbirth? What does having a baby mean to you?

"When Elizabeth heard Mary's greeting, the child leaped in her womb. And Elizabeth was filled with the Holy Spirit . . ."
—Luke 1:41

How did you feel the first time you felt your baby move? The very first time, I wasn't completely sure that funny feeling in my stomach was the flutter of a baby. Maybe it was a gas bubble. Maybe I was just imagining things. Soon, however, there was no doubt. The tickling feeling that raced across the inside of my belly was my baby in action. Often I couldn't help smiling when I felt it.

Elizabeth was beginning the sixth month of her pregnancy when Mary came visiting, so she had probably felt her baby's movements many times. She probably already knew the patterns of her baby's activity. If her baby was like mine, he probably dozed while her workaday movements gently rocked him and then sprang into action when she lay down to rest! Maybe she had begun talking to her long-awaited child. In any case, her unborn baby could hear her voice when she spoke to others or sang as she went about her work.

One day something unusual happened. Elizabeth received an unexpected visitor, her young relative Mary. Mary had barely said hello when Elizabeth's baby leapt in her womb. An unborn baby was the first human being to respond to the good news Mary carried in her heart! A pregnant woman was the first person to put that response into words: Elizabeth was filled with the Holy Spirit and broke out in words of blessing. She boldly interpreted her baby's movement as a leap of joy that the Messiah was soon to be born.

You don't have to be an Elizabeth or a Mary to sense the

Spirit's nearness during pregnancy. Many women feel that they live and move in a special state of grace while they're pregnant. And why not? After all, you play a central role in an unfolding miracle. Your baby's leaps and bounds remind you daily (and nightly) that you bear within you a whole new human being! I like a good night's sleep as much as anyone. Still, even the nightly interruptions were a small price to pay for those wonderful sensations.

We have barely begun to explore and describe the grace-filled dimensions of being pregnant. Maybe we take them for granted. Still, something special and life-affirming surrounds and fills us while we're pregnant. Psychologists note that pregnant women seem to wear invisible armor against suicide, in spite of their increased tendency to mood swings.

Even women for whom pregnancy poses definite practical problems often find themselves buoyed up in spite of their difficulties. Check out Maya Angelou's *I Know Why the Caged Bird Sings*, for example. In it, Angelou tells about her own unwed pregnancy at age sixteen. Ashamed and frightened, she managed to hide her pregnancy until she graduated from high school—eight months pregnant! Strangely, as she played the part of a carefree schoolgirl, she "very nearly caught the essence of teenage capriciousness. . . . School recovered its lost magic. For the first time [in a long time] information was exciting for itself alone." Why such new reactions? "During what surely must have been a critical period I was not dragged down by hopelessness."

Where do you feel grace lifting and blessing your own pregnancy? Perhaps you love the wonderful pleasure of feeling life stirring within you. Perhaps your spirits are lifted by the hope that a growing new baby represents. Perhaps you enjoy the shared pleasure of guiding your husband's hands along your abdomen so he, too, can feel your baby's kicks and leaps. Perhaps you enjoy the new sense of community—even complete strangers often feel they have a stake in an unborn child. Their pats to my stomach, and unsolicited advice occasionally annoyed me. Most of the time, though, I enjoyed people reaching out to me through the shell of reserve that usually separates us from one another.

Enjoy these times, and store them in your heart. Jot insights down in your prayer journal so you can turn to them for inspiration at times when life seems difficult. If you have a hard time rejoicing at your baby's movements and growing presence in your life, bring that, too, to God in prayer. Troubles or sorrow may overshadow your enjoyment of your pregnancy, but they can't chase away God's spirit.

Remember that the good news that set Elizabeth's unborn baby leaping for joy is good news for all of us—every moment of every day. The Christ who took form in Mary's womb will hold you up through all that life has to offer—its trials as well as its joys.

Dear Jesus, thank you for being born of a human mother, just like all the rest of us. Thank you for caring for me and standing by me. Thank you for laughing with me when I'm happy and weeping with me when I'm down. Thank you for sending your spirit to lift and inspire me. Help me enjoy my growing baby's movements now. Help me remember the joy of these moments when I face hurdles down the road. Amen.

✦ What do you enjoy most about being pregnant? What do you find most troublesome? Where do you see the grace of God in your pregnancy?

"Just as you do not know how the breath comes to the bones in the mother's womb, so you do not know the work of God, who makes everything."
—Ecclesiastes 11:5

Just how does breath come to the bones in a mother's womb? You can read about fetal development, and imagine what your baby looks like at this stage of your pregnancy. You can make an educated guess about how much its internal organs have developed. But who can really explain how breath comes to the bones? Who can explain just what makes the complicated process click?

Birth has always fascinated human beings. Early peoples had various theories of what was going on deep in the womb. Some saw it as basically a female process and viewed the moon as responsible for a woman's pregnancy. Others saw it as a male process in which the woman served passively, like a field in which the man planted seed.

The Bible, too, explores the mystery of pregnancy and birth. Job 10:9-11 contains a mini-tour of biblical views. In this short space, Job likens God to a potter who forms him out of clay, a dairymaid who pours out milk and curdles it, and a clothesmaker who knits together bones and sinews and who clothes the embryo with flesh and skin.

Job isn't trying to write a biology textbook. He uses these varied pictures to say something important about God: God makes birth possible in ways that we can only begin to imagine. God is the hidden third partner in each and every pregnancy. What looks to us like a father depositing his semen in a woman's womb is God pouring out a little milk. What looks to us like the woman's womb transforming that liquid into something solid is God producing a human curd. For all its insightful imagery, the Bible leaves the details of birth veiled in mystery. Indeed, Ecclesiastes points to the mystery of birth as a sign of the still greater mystery of God's awesome work in all creation.

Modern science has explained much about the process of conception and birth. Today we know that both the woman's egg and the man's sperm are actively involved in conception. Scientists have developed "windows" into the womb that allow us to check on our babies while they are still deep inside our bodies: An ultrasound scan, for example, can give you a blurry black-and-white glimpse of your baby's shape and movements. Not only can we peer into the womb, we can also observe conception outside the womb: Today egg and sperm can join in a laboratory dish and then go on to thrive in a woman's womb.

Does our new knowledge lessen God's creative work? I don't think so. The more I learn about the delicate interactions involved in the birth process, the more amazing I find the created splendor of it all. The more that human insight and ingenuity lead to new understanding and healing procedures, the more I marvel at the brains God gave us.

Still mysteries remain. We don't know why fertility procedures work some of the time but not all the time. (Only half of the couples who pursue fertility treatment conceive.) For that matter, we don't know why so many seemingly infertile couples go on to get pregnant. (One-third do so without any medical help.) Mysteries also remain about what sets the birth process in motion. Does the mother start the process, or does the child, or what? Believe me, you may wonder about that a lot—especially if your pregnancy goes much beyond your due date! I wondered plenty about that question during my first pregnancy, especially by the end of my second week "overdue"!

Both our knowledge and its limits present spiritual opportunities. The things we know can help us praise. One of my favorite hymns starts with these words: "Arise, all things that God has made; arise and praise God's glory!" The hymn's ten verses lead a merry tour through creation, taking time to wonder at everything from a blade of grass to the starry heavens. The hymn writer even imagines looking into the mouths of the many fish swimming deep in the ocean! The hymn catalogs creation—in order to praise God. The more detailed our catalog and understanding of creation, the better we can praise the Creator.

At the same time, our increasing scientific knowledge challenges us to exercise our spiritual gifts. New technologies keep spilling forth, and they all have their pros and cons. Even a process as normal as childbearing has become high-tech business. Think carefully about the tests you are offered. Ask about the equipment and procedures that you may meet in the hospital. Decide in advance what level of technological assistance you think is best, then prepare your mind and body accordingly.

Finally, remember that the limits of our knowledge also present a spiritual opportunity. Some cultures keep women in the dark about the birth process—talking about birth is taboo. Women in these cultures approach birth with fear, but they also seem to get a sense of cosmic participation out of it. We know a lot about birth, and we need not approach birth with such great fear. Still, we don't know everything, and we can't control everything. In childbirth we, too, plunge into the great mysteries of life and death. We stretch and meet our limits. Hopefully this process will help us appreciate and trust our bodies. Hopefully, too, it will help us draw closer to the creative, strong, and loving God who made us.

Dear God, thank you for giving me a body that can bear children. Thank you for giving me a mind that can understand many things. Thank you for giving me a heart that can love and make wise decisions. Thank you for all of life's wonders, and for the mystery and majesty that boggles our minds. Help me trust you as I face the unknown; help me praise you through all I know and do. Amen.

✦ How do you imagine God working in the womb? What new insights does your pregnancy give you into God's creative work?

*"For it was you who formed my inward parts;
you knit me together in my mother's womb. I praise you,
for I am fearfully and wonderfully made."
—Psalm 139:13,14*

Have you begun gathering tiny sleepers and bibs and blankets? Maybe friends have begun showering you with baby things or lending you little outfits their own children have outgrown. Pregnancy gives you a chance to make practical preparations for your baby's arrival. You have time now to gather baby clothes and furniture and equipment. Some women start this nesting process early in their pregnancy. Others put it off until they feel sure their baby is well along the way.

The first time I was pregnant, I even managed to knit a little sweater for the baby growing inside me. Evenings I sat knitting in my rocking chair, just like my idealized picture of a pregnant woman. I enjoyed those hours—dreaming and chatting with my husband to the soft click of the knitting needles, watching the balls of yarn slowly turn into little sleeves, and miniature back and front pieces. Occasionally I made a mistake and had to go back and redo something. Even so, I found the work meaningful and satisfying; the work of my hands paralleled the creative work of my womb.

While you knit, shop for and prepare for your baby, God knits, too. And with God there are no dropped stitches, no overpriced goods, no assembly-line clones. God has knit together millions of babies. Still, each is unique and priceless;

each is precious in God's sight. As the psalmist says in response to God's handiwork, "I praise you, for I am fearfully and wonderfully made."

You and God are in this together. God gave you a body able to nourish and protect your baby. God works with you in the hidden reaches of your womb to produce your beautiful baby. You do your part in many ways. You eat well and exercise to help your body do its job. You pray for your baby's health. You gather diapers and clothes. You make room in your heart and your home for the little newcomer.

We don't know just how God works in your womb. Ultrasound scans can't catch God's fingers in the act of forming your child. Stethoscopes can't pick up the click of God's knitting needles. The most advanced medical technology comes up short: only the eyes of faith can catch a glimpse of God's womb work. What do such eyes see? The psalmist shows us that God's creative work resembles our own. God, too, takes time to lovingly knit quality goods. God, too, enjoys the satisfaction of finishing a superior piece of work.

The psalmist also shows us that God's "womb work" confounds human categories. In one verse God knits the baby together in its mother's womb. In the next, God sees the baby being finely woven or embroidered in the depths of the earth. You and I may not be able to be in two places at one time, but no such limits cramp God's babymaking style!

However God does it, the point is this: The miracle happening in your womb is more than a personal and family affair. It connects you to God and to the profound mystery of all life. The miracle going on in your womb is somehow woven together in the depths of the earth—you and your baby are intimately connected to all creation!

When I imagine God embroidering baby's finishing touches in the depths of the earth, I'm reminded of a dainty bib that my grandmother made. She embroidered it and edged it with lace for her first grandchild's baptism many years ago. Since then, the bib has protected several baptismal gowns. Now I have it tucked safely away until the day I can pass it on into the next generation.

None of us sees all the preparations being made for our baby. None of us can completely grasp all the connections that link us to the rest of creation. The unseen efforts of past generations provide building materials for your nest today. The earth nourishes you and your baby with its fruits. God knits and embroiders and inspires.

Your womb partnership with God produces a baby for you to love and care for. Your shared love and responsibility for that child provides another strand in the fabric of your life—a strand that can knit you closer to God, to your family, and to all creation.

Dear God, thanks for making me your partner. Help me feel your presence as I make practical preparations for our baby. Help me enjoy gathering things the baby will need—and keep me from getting bogged down in the things I think I have to have. Help me see how my family and I fit into the tapestry of life that you weave with us. Amen.

✦ How do you feel about being a partner in God's creative work? Think of ways you and your baby are connected to the rest of creation.

"Did not [God] who made me in the womb make them? And did not one fashion us in the womb? . . . from my youth I reared the orphan like a father, and from my mother's womb I guided the widow."
—Job 31:15, 18

Parenthood can sure open your eyes. For example, I didn't give much thought to the level of violence on television until I had small children in the house. Suddenly I began to see the world through their young eyes—and I saw lots of grim stuff. No wonder parents have banded together to pressure television executives to provide healthier programming!

Perhaps you have already begun to see the world with your child in mind. You may have become more aware of the dangers that threaten people even if they live relatively safe lives. If such thoughts trouble you, take heart—many pregnant women experience similar fears, and they typically diminish when the baby is born. In the meantime, accept your fears and learn from them. A little fear can be a healthy thing: We have good reasons for teaching our children to fear electrical sockets and open flames. The fears that may trouble you during pregnancy can remind you that we are vulnerable creatures—in spite of all our security systems and insurance policies. We need one another and we need God.

The child blossoming in your womb can give you new eyes in other ways, too. Perhaps you feel a special new connection to every baby you see. Even the young of other species may tug at your heartstrings: puppies, kittens, chicks, you name it. Of course you don't have to be pregnant for your heart to reach out to innocent and vulnerable little beings. Still, pregnancy may bring out maternal instincts you didn't know you had.

Job reminds us that God feels motherly tenderness and concern for everyone—rich or poor, young or old. After all, God fashioned each of us in our mother's womb. God fashions your baby and the baby of a poor African woman who has barely enough to eat. God fashions the baby of the most famous Hollywood star and the baby of your humblest neighbor. God has a parent's interest in each one of us. That means we are all related through God—and when the chips are down, family members help one another. Thus Job made a point of treating the neighbor's orphan as his own child; he advised a neighboring widow just as he would his own mother. God works through each of us to care for all God's children.

As time goes on, you'll get plenty of opportunities to work with God to make the world more child-friendly. Perhaps you already teach Sunday school or help with the nursery at your church. Perhaps you already do your part to improve your neighborhood and try to provide a good role model at work. Even so, parenthood can give you new incentive and a longer-term vision. The future world citizen you carry in your belly gives you a special stake in the future. No wonder parents often function as "pillars of society": Children tend to focus the mind and energies on long-term basics—good schools, safe communities, stable relationships.

Before you start feeling too much like a pillar, however, let me point out that pregnancy and parenthood bring a glorious topsy-turviness into life, too. You're probably already changing your habits to accommodate prenatal appointments, childbirth classes, and your bulging tummy and cramped bladder. After your baby is born, your customary schedules will probably fly out the window. As I recall, day blurred into night for weeks. For a while I wondered if we'd ever again be able to finish a meal without being interrupted!

We did eventually manage to finish meals in relative peace. Your life, too, will settle into a new rhythm. Those weeks of topsy-turvy transition serve a healthy purpose. They jostle us out of our routines; they call us to start anew.

Every pregnancy shakes life up a bit. Mary's turned the whole world upside down! She burst out in exultation, "My soul magnifies the Lord . . . he has put down the mighty from their thrones, and exalted those of low degree; he has filled the hungry with good things, and the rich he has sent away empty." In her pregnancy, Mary saw God turning the world upside down in order to bring justice to all!

God worked through Mary and her son; God works through you, and me, and our children. God counts on each of us and blesses our efforts to make the world a happier and healthier home for all.

Dear God, help me through the dangers and difficulties I face. Give me the confidence and patience to deal with uncertainty and change. Show me how to make the world a little healthier and happier—for my baby and for all your beloved children.

✦ Has your pregnancy changed anything about the way you look at the world? What, if anything, do you see in a new light?

6

God with Us

"Before the mountains were born, before Thou didst give birth to the earth and the world, Even from everlasting to everlasting Thou art God."
—Psalm 90:2 (NASB)

Imagine God conceiving of the whole vast wonderful universe. Imagine God musing over how the stars should shine and how the planets would move in their orbits. Imagine God travailing all alone to bring forth our beautiful planet, with its imposing mountains and fertile valleys, its vast oceans and plains. What a creative, strong God it took to bring such a creation to birth!

This same God has laid similar strength and creativity into the fibers of your being. Remember that on days when you feel as if you're carrying a mountain around in front of you. Fortunately you and I don't have to bring forth real mountains! Still, carrying a good-sized baby and its water bed around with you all the time takes energy. Find time to put your feet up, rest, and muse a bit. Take time for physical exercise, too—especially if your daily routine involves lots of sitting or standing still. Stretching exercises, swimming, biking, or other light exercise can help you relax and increase your stamina and strength.

Most modern women need to plan exercise into their schedules—in contrast to the generations of our foremothers whose daily life involved much physical labor. These women built up strength and stamina that stood them in good stead when they gave birth. Tribal women from Greenland to the Kalahari Desert amazed European explorers with their ability to give birth quickly and then to get on with their work. Danish explorer Peter Freuchen told about giving an Eskimo woman some skins to prepare one morning. "She brought them back in the afternoon deploring that it had taken so long, but she had had a baby in the meantime!" Similarly, the story of Moses' birth suggests that Hebrew slave women's birthing labors went very fast. The Hebrew midwives told Pharaoh that, unlike the delicate Egyptian women, Hebrew women "are of lively stock; they give birth before the midwife comes to them" (Exodus 1:19, author's translation).

If you have not already done so, begin now to exercise your blooming body in preparation for childbirth. God has given you strong muscles, flexibility, and endurance. Still, like an athlete, you can bring out the best in what God has given you. Your midwife, doctor, or childbirth class instructor may already have recommended a set of exercises to improve your body's strength and your ability to relax. On the other hand, if you haven't yet heard about "kegels" and the like, look for a copy of Elizabeth Noble's *Essential Exercises for the Childbearing Year.* Noble explains how you can improve your physical well-being both before and after giving birth.

Exercise your spirit as you exercise your body. Pray while you exercise: A simple repetitive prayer can enhance your breathing and stretching exercises. You may want to try the classic Jesus prayer. Centuries ago a monk tried to figure out how to pray ceaselessly, as the Bible tells us to do. He came up with a prayer designed to match the rhythms of breathing. It goes like this: Pray "Lord Jesus Christ, Son of God" as you slowly take air in, and "have mercy on me a sinner" as you slowly breathe out. You might want to vary this prayer with one inspired by Psalm 90:

"Gracious God, who gave birth to the world" as you breathe in; "grant me a heart of wisdom" as you breathe out.

You can also weave your physical efforts into a thankful prayer: Note and celebrate even the tiniest improvements in your strength and stamina. Remember times when you have experienced your own strength—whether it was while running a race, completing a project that was hard to do, or summoning up the courage to say words that needed to be said. Pay attention to the well of strength God has given you. The God who brings forth mountains gives you strength and courage, too.

Even the best exercise regimen can't guarantee a quick and smooth birth. Still, the daily discipline of developing your muscles and lungs will strengthen your physical and spiritual ability to deal with whatever surprises your labor brings. I exercised quite faithfully during my first pregnancy—and never had a chance to use my breathing techniques or test my physical prowess. My waters broke and were stained with meconium that would not be good for my baby's lungs. We waited for hours—still no contractions. Finally I was wheeled into the operating room. All those exercises and breathing routines had been a waste—or had they? As I lay waiting for the surgeons to do their job, my husband leaned over and whispered to me, "I never knew you were so strong." He wasn't talking about physical strength; my body wasn't in a position to show what my muscles could do. He saw strength of spirit—strength that had built up over a lifetime, strength that increased as I prayed through my bending and stretching. That strength, like your strength, comes from the God who gave birth to mountains, the God who knows birth inside out.

Dear God, thank you for giving me a capable body and spirit. Help me grow stronger and more confident through my pregnancy. Help me live every day filled with confidence in your strength and love. In Jesus' name, Amen.

✦ Try to imagine God giving birth to the earth and the world. What does this picture tell you about God? Explore your own God-given strengths, both physical and spiritual.

"'Look, the virgin shall conceive and bear a son, and they shall name him 'Emmanuel,' which means 'God is with us.'"
—Matthew 1:23

"Oh yuck! Did I look like that?" A few pages later: "What is that gunk all over it?" So much for Lennart Nilsson's exquisitely beautiful photographs of human fetuses nestled deep within their mother's wombs and babies freshly emerged from their mothers' bodies. From a youngster's perspective the embryo's head looks grotesquely large; the newborn's protective coating of skin grease, streaked with blood, looks like a mess. Even when it takes place in the most sterile surroundings, birth remains a messy, blood-and-guts affair as well as a sublime, gloriously creative experience.

Viewed from the outside, pregnancy, birthing, and even the sex act itself can seem disturbingly messy and animal-like. You may have heard the story of the boy who asked his mother how the baby she was expecting got into her tummy in the first place. She described as simply and matter-of-factly as she could how Daddy had entered her body. "Is that how you made Tony and me, too?" her son asked.

"Yes," she answered, "that's how babies get started."

"You mean you did that three times! You must have wanted us pretty bad!"

Today sex is not unmentionable as it once was. Today few pregnant women go into hiding as soon as they begin to show. You may even find it hard to believe that women who lived a hundred years ago often felt intense shame about their pregnant bodies. Nice women were expected to confine themselves to their homes until the baby was born. Still, we haven't completely rid ourselves of the notion that there is something dirty about sex. We all know that a dirty joke is not a funny story about making mud pies, and a dirty old man isn't an elderly gentleman who needs a bath.

The connection between sexual processes and uncleanness was much stronger in Jesus' day. The Hebrew Bible, especially the book of Leviticus, contains very specific rules about religious cleanness. Some of these rules warn that menstruation, ejaculation, intercourse, and childbirth all make a person "unclean." They then outline specific remedies for the situation. This uncleanness has little to do with the messiness of flowing blood and semen. Rather these rules express awe. Sex, like death, brings human beings dangerously close to the life-giving power and mystery of the divine. No wonder cultures around the world have rules and taboos intended to protect people from the full force of that power.

Unfortunately such taboos can leave the impression that sex is dirty or shameful. How wonderful, then, that God was not above entering into the mess and danger of being born human. God-in-Christ bent, stretched, and grew in a woman's womb. God-in-Christ made the scary trip through the birth canal, then emerged streaked with the blood and "gunk" of birth. God's birth in Christ gives new dignity to every human birth.

Even so, you may sometimes feel embarrassed about carrying around such obvious evidence of your sex life. Even if you are proud to be pregnant, you may dislike regularly exposing your bottom in your doctor's office. Few of us like to have strangers poke around in our private parts.

Pregnancy exposes your body to the world in many new ways. How do you feel about that? You may feel vulnerable and embarrassed by all the attention to your sexual organs. On the other hand, you may be so interested in your changing body that you look forward to your checkups. You may even find that the frequent physical exams become routine and that you start taking inspection of your body more matter-of-factly.

Whatever your feelings, accept and explore them. They can put you in touch with your own sense of modesty. Modesty may sound like an old-fashioned virtue today. I think, however, that your sense of modesty reflects your humanity. If you were a pure spirit like the angels, you wouldn't have a body to show or modestly hide. If you were simply a body, you'd follow your instincts as publicly as any other animal. You are a human, though. That means that you are an embodied spirit and a spirit-filled body whose sense of modesty seeks to set fitting limits. One of the challenges of pregnancy is to set new limits that show more of yourself and still retain your personal dignity.

Equally important, pregnancy challenges you to accept your body in its weakness and in its strength, in its elegance and in its messiness. Pregnancy can help you marvel at all the intricate changes your body makes in order to pass life on. Childbearing can help you see the protective, creamy beauty in the "gunk" coating a newborn's skin.

As you go about sorting out your feelings and coming to terms with your body, remember that God is with you. God came into the world in the person of Jesus. God came to share in our humanness and to redeem us from the sin and shame that mess us up. God came into the world in Jesus, who is also called Emmanuel. And "Emmanuel," as the angel pointed out, means "God is with us." Thanks to Jesus, you can trust that God knows birth from the inside out, and that God is indeed with us, even to the extremes of whatever life and death may bring.

Dear Jesus, thank you for coming into the world and showing once and for all that God is with us, even in life's most extreme situations. Help me accept my body. Help me keep my sense of worth and dignity, even when I have my legs up in stirrups. Amen.

✦ How has the increasing exposure and examination of your body affected your sense of modesty? How do you think you will deal with the exposure that goes along with giving birth?

"You were unmindful of the Rock who bore you;
you forgot the God who gave you birth."
—Deuteronomy 32:18

"That young fella is really a chip off the old block, isn't he!" Friends and relatives will soon be scrutinizing your baby's face, trying to decide who he or she looks like. As soon as it is born, your baby will begin imitating your facial expressions. If you watch your husband make faces to your child while he or she is quiet and alert shortly after birth, you may well see your baby mimic Papa. Before long, you'll see your child picking up many familiar mannerisms. Daddy's favored phrases will start popping up in conversation in your child's high voice. You'll see your own gestures performed by chubby toddler arms.

We give our children so much of ourselves. You and your mate have already given your child its very own, individual set of genes. The color of your child's eyes and skin, the shape of her nose, the size of his feet—the building plans for these details and many more have already been laid down in your child's cells. Part of the fun of watching your child develop and grow will be seeing family traits emerge in new combinations.

It takes more than genes to make a baby, of course. During

pregnancy you also give your child some of your body space and strength. The food you eat no longer goes entirely to repairing and fueling your own body. You share every morsel you eat with the fetus growing inside you. I loved knowing that. For one thing, I could eat more good food without it turning into useless fat! Moreover, I felt a growing bond with my baby as I ate for both of us. Even Communion took on new meaning. We can't see just how morsels of bread and wine become Christ's body and blood, but we know that we arise from the table strengthened in faith. You can't see how your body transforms food into energy and passes it on in appropriate amounts to your baby, but you see your belly swelling and know your baby is growing. Who knows, maybe the body and blood of Christ that strengthens you passes right on through your placenta and into your baby's budding soul. I like to think so.

In any case, we give our children much more than genes and physical nourishment. Even now you give your baby the comforting sound of your heartbeat and a familiar voice. Maybe you sing to your baby—women in many cultures make a point of doing so. Babies can hear from inside the womb as early as the fourth or fifth month of pregnancy. The baby's father can share his musical gifts with your unborn child, too. Your newborn may delight both of you by recognizing tunes it heard from within your womb.

As time goes on, you will share your home, your love, your interests, and your values with your child. Parents and grandparents enjoy much of this giving—seeing your child's face light up with joy is such a precious gift. Even busy career people often lose track of time watching their children explore and play, imitate their folks, and try new things.

Enjoyable as this giving may be, it does involve some sacrifice. Your body undergoes considerable stress during pregnancy. The amount of stress varies from woman to woman and pregnancy to pregnancy, but all of us lose some energy and mobility. At the very least your muscles get stretched and your lungs, heart, and kidneys all have to work overtime. Someone once warned me that you lose a tooth for every baby. That shouldn't happen if you pay attention to your teeth and gums during pregnancy. Still that old tale points out that pregnancy, for all its joys, does take its toll on your body. Take good care of yourself so that you have strength to share!

Where do you find the physical and spiritual strength it takes to bear and raise a child? Moses calls attention to the Rock who bore us, the God who gave us birth. We are all chips off the old block, so to speak—drawing our life, energy, and ability to love from the God who gave us life and continues to uplift and nourish us. God is as stable and strong as a rock, and at the same time as self-giving and passionate as a mother. You are blessed by the God who provides unlimited strength. This same God rejoices to see you grow in grace and wisdom. So lean on the Rock, remember the God who gave us all birth, and show your resemblance to the God who loves you.

Dear God, thank you for giving me the solid foundation of your love. Help me share my love with my baby, even as I share my body, my food, my breath, and my songs. Help me rely on you as completely as my unborn baby relies on me. In Jesus' name, Amen.

✦ How do you feel about sharing your body with your child? Where do you find the physical and spiritual resources to share yourself? Who or what does God work through to uplift and nourish you?

"We know that the whole creation has been groaning together and travailing together until now; and not only the creation, but we ourselves, who have the first fruits of the Spirit, groan inwardly while we wait for adoption, the redemption of our bodies. . . . the Spirit helps us in our weakness; for we do not know how to pray as we ought, but that very Spirit intercedes with sighs too deep for words."
—Romans 8:22 f.,26 (author's translation)

"Are we there yet? How much longer before we get there?" You'll probably hear those questions many times in the course of your mothering days. Time spent traveling toward a special destination can seem like an eternity—for youngsters, and for all of us.

Right now your own journey toward Birth Day may seem awfully long. Most of the first surprise and excitement has worn off. There's no longer any doubt in your mind that there really is a baby in there! By this time you may be so used to being pregnant that your pre-pregnant days seem very long ago and far away. If your pregnancy has been difficult, you may long to get it over with. Even if you love being pregnant, you may be getting impatient to meet the baby you have carried within you for so long.

In any case, your pregnancy will soon enter the home stretch. Soon your doctor or midwife will ask you to come for a checkup every other week rather than once a month. Maybe you've started to make lists of things to do before the baby arrives.

How do you feel about this waiting time? Maybe time seems to drag on as it does for children counting the days until their next birthday. Maybe you feel it passes altogether too quickly, like it does when you're trying to get all your Christmas preparations done in time. Maybe you have mixed emotions—both wanting to hold onto this special time, and eager to get your baby in your hands; or tired of waiting, but not quite ready to meet the challenges of labor and delivery.

Few of us enjoy waiting. We like to call the shots and do things at our own pace. Waiting in line, waiting in a doctor's office, waiting for the bus to come—waiting means someone else sets the schedule. When you're pregnant, God and your body set the schedule. You can't hurry the process much, but you can make the most of the waiting.

Waiting gives you time to figure out where the baby will sleep and what it will wear. It gives you time to dream dreams and make plans with the baby's father. It gives you time to prepare your older children for a new sibling and to make arrangements regarding employment. It gives you time to make room in your heart and your life and to start seeing yourself in a new role. The waiting of pregnancy can put you in tune with your body. While I was pregnant, I paid more attention than ever before to my body and its rhythms. The waiting of pregnancy provides time to meditate and an occasion to stretch your spirit. What a magnificent glimpse of God's creative plan in action!

Indeed, the waiting of pregnancy can put you in tune with all creation. If you ever start thinking that nine months is a long time to wait, think of the creation. The apostle Paul writes that creation has been *travailing* (not just expecting!) since sin entered the world so long ago. The good news is that all that waiting and groaning and travailing came to fruition in the person of Jesus Christ.

The waiting of pregnancy is much like the Christian life. You have your baby already. You can feel it kick and stretch, maybe you even feel it hiccup! We have Jesus already, too. We can already enjoy the first fruits of the Spirit. We received them at our baptism. Thus we know that we are God's children, as surely as we know the child in our womb is alive and kicking, and that it is flesh of our flesh. The Spirit assures us that we are indeed God's children, and still we await the day when God will make this plain for all to see. We look forward to God redeeming our bodies from death and decay. We look forward to God lifting us up and taking us home.

As Christians wait to see God face to face, you wait now to see your child face to face. You long to see for yourself that your baby is healthy. I remember praying intensely that my baby would be born healthy—not because I suspected otherwise, but because there is always an element of uncertainty in the unknown. We don't know everything. We can't see everything. We don't even know how to pray as we ought. Thank God for the Spirit, who helps us to do what we can't manage on our own! Paul assures us that the Spirit will help us pray as we ought. The Spirit will express what is in our hearts—with sighs too deep for words. A birthing woman sighs and groans in her creative labors; so, too, the Spirit sighs with and for us, out of the depths of creative love.

However long you have to wait to see your child face to face, know that the Spirit will hang in there with you. When Birth Day finally arrives, the Spirit will stay with you and help you. The Spirit will stand by you through the ups and downs of parenthood. However long your life turns out to be, however many ups and downs you meet along the way, the Spirit will stand by you as you wait to see God face to face.

Dear Jesus, thank you for sending the Holy Spirit to help and encourage me. You know it can be hard to wait. Please give me a sense of your peace so that I can enjoy the waiting. Give me patience and confidence, and help me grow ever closer to you. Amen.

✦ How do you take the waiting that is part of pregnancy?

"For a long time I have held my peace,
I have kept still and restrained myself; now I will cry
out like a woman in labor, I will gasp and pant."
—Isaiah 42:14

Every once in a while you hear stories of women who get through pregnancy and childbirth without missing a beat. There was the pastor who preached her Sunday sermon in the midst of labor contractions. There was the student who delivered her baby over spring break—and was back in class when school started again. And then there was the outdoors woman who didn't let the advanced stage of her pregnancy stop her from going on one last wilderness trip with her husband.

Our foremothers may have felt they had to confine themselves to their homes when they were "in the family way." Today's women are more likely to feel they must prove that pregnancy doesn't cramp their style or their ability to function in the workplace.

What is your ideal? Do you like the idea of slowing down and cutting out extra obligations so that you can focus on this special time in your life? Or do you take pride in doing everything you usually do? Maybe you feel mixed emotions—ready to bag your job one day, proud of how well you cope the next. Don't be too hard on yourself if you find you can't accomplish tasks as quickly as you could before. After all, you are doing very important work, even when you don't lift a finger. Making a baby takes time and energy that doesn't show up on any work schedule. On the other hand, if you need and want to, you may be able to carry on almost as usual until it's time to deliver. Many of us are stronger than we think.

However you feel, remember that God is in this with you. God is with you as you try to find a balance that works for you.

God is with you as you make plans, deal with mixed feelings, and learn to roll with the punches. God will be with you when you feel the first contractions and when you push your baby out.

Indeed, the prophet Isaiah tells us that God knows what it feels like to give birth. I love this picture of God in the midst of birthing labor: She is so strong, so creative, so dynamic. She knows what it feels like to hold the distress and promise in for a time. She also knows how to let loose with loud cries when the final, tumultuous birth pangs are upon her. We human beings are created in the image of this strong, creative, loving God: Remember her, and draw strength from her when you need it.

The divine birthing labor Isaiah pictured lasted a long time—in the meantime a whole generation of Israelites lived and died as prisoners of war in Babylon. They wondered if they had lost God along with their homeland. They wondered where God was while they suffered. All the while God was as close to them as you are to your unborn child. All the while God suffered with her people, bearing her birth pangs in silence. If you sometimes wonder where God is, and have a hard time hearing God's voice, remember the story of those Israelites. Remember that even when God seems very far away, God envelopes you and nourishes you—just as you envelop and nourish your growing child.

The first time I read Isaiah's description of God giving birth I imagined God striding back and forth on the stage of history, purposefully doing her creative work. Since then, I have given birth myself three times. I no longer imagine God striding quite so briskly back and forth. I no longer imagine God as some kind of superwoman who sails through pregnancy and the throes of labor without being affected by it. God suffers with us when we hurt. God suffers in silence when we reap the results of our carelessness and blindness. Still, when the time is right, God lets loose that birthing cry and turns creation upside down to make way for new life. This is the God who gives us power to endure suffering, the God who gives us strength to bring forth new life, the God who shows us how to let loose our own creative love.

Dear God, thank you for the strength and creative power of my body. Thank you for giving me a spirit that seeks you. You know what it is like to give birth: help me take my pregnancy in stride. Lift me up when I feel tired or down. Cheer me on when I test my strength and endurance. In Jesus' name. Amen.

✦ Can you imagine God giving birth? How does that picture affect you?

"O Lord, my heart is not lifted up, my eyes are not raised too high; I do not occupy myself with things too great and too marvelous for me. But I have calmed and quieted my soul, like a child quieted at it mother's breast; like a child that is quieted is my soul."
—Psalm 131:1f.

Babies thrive on cuddling. Recent research has found that even premature babies, who need to spend most of their time in an incubator, do better if they also receive skin-to-skin contact from their parents. Right now your womb takes care of that cuddling automatically. Soon you will have a chance to take your baby to your breast, to feel its soft skin and searching little mouth, to hear its heartbeat and its breathing, its newborn cries for help and its contented sucking.

Both parents can and do cuddle their child. Still, the picture of a mother holding her baby touches hearts in a special way. Over the centuries, Christian artists have portrayed Mary with baby Jesus thousands of times. Generations have loved these pictures; they radiate such peace and joy. In recent years I have heard rumors that the post office is thinking about limiting its holiday stamps to general themes—Santas and snowmen instead of Madonna and child. So far that hasn't happened. People have insisted that the beautiful pictures of Madonna and child continue to have a place in our hearts and on our holiday mail.

I'm less familiar with the art of other cultures, but I suspect they include depictions of mother and child, too. The bond between mother and child is a basic element of human life; it spans the cultures. You may already have heard about the importance of bonding with your newborn. Many childbirth educators emphasize the importance of looking into your baby's eyes, exploring its body, and feeling its skin on yours immediately after it is born. Talk to your doctor or midwife to make plans for some quiet and relaxed time for you and your newborn to get acquainted. Don't worry about how to go about bonding; if you have a peaceful setting, instinct will take care of the rest.

God created us ready to bond. You have instincts that will lead you to touch and talk to your infant; your infant's cry will trigger your hormones to set your milk flowing. Your baby is born ready to bond to you, too. Its little mouth will seek out your breast, although it has never tasted food before. Once it has found your breast, it will see your face clearly. Newborn babies see best at a distance of eight to ten inches—about the distance from baby's face to yours while you nurse. Objects that are closer or farther away go out of focus.

God created us with a lifelong need to bond with other people. Adults, too, need others to nourish them, comfort them, and play with them. During your pregnancy you may feel a greater than usual need to be mothered and cuddled and comforted. There may be days when you feel overwhelmed by all you're going through and all that the future will bring. Even the most responsible adults occasionally need a strong shoulder to lean on or a listening ear to bend. Feel free to ask for the attention you need.

You may have a hard time accepting the needy child in yourself. Even children don't like to feel dependent: Before you know it, your little one will be telling you, "I can do it myself!" Now that you're an adult, you may find it hard to graciously receive the help people offer. Maybe you feel guilty taking help you could get by without; maybe your pride gets in the way. Even if you don't ask for it, enjoy the tender loving care your family, your friends, and even strangers may offer. Of course you can still manage to open doors for yourself, but those around you may like to show their support by pampering you a bit.

God created us with a lifelong desire to bond with one another. God also gave us a yearning to bond with our creator. King David understood this when he wrote, "I have calmed and quieted my soul, like a child quieted at its mother's breast." Fame and power couldn't quiet King David's soul; a close relationship with God could. He pictures his soul as a helpless child snuggling up to God. This beloved child doesn't look far afield. Rather he focuses on the nearby face of the God who cuddles, nourishes, and protects him.

God is with you, too. God will help you and sustain you. God will listen to your cries and comfort you. God will feed you the pure spiritual milk you need to grow in grace. God will give you the peace and confidence you need to live life to the fullest.

Dear God, thank you for creating us to love one another. Protect the child I carry in my womb; protect the child I am. Give me strength and courage to meet life's challenges. Help my eyes focus on your loving presence in my life. Feed me with the pure spiritual milk, that I may feed those who depend on me. In Jesus' name, Amen.

✦ Can you imagine God as a mother cuddling you to her breast? What does that picture tell you about God and about yourself?

7

The Shadowside of Childbirth

"The children struggled together within [Rebekah]; and she said, 'If it is to be this way, why do I live?' So she went to inquire of the Lord."
—Genesis 25:22-23

Congratulations—you've entered the final stretch! Just a few more weeks and you'll be able to see your baby face to face. Up until now, your baby has been able to move quite freely in your womb. It could even turn somersaults inside you. By the seventh month, though, most of your womb's available space is used up. No more somersaults for a while! Your baby will have to make do with stretching, kicking, and jostling around for the time being.

With so much baby packed into your belly, you may start feeling less comfortable, too. The more your baby grows, the more your lungs and bladder feel the squeeze. You may find it increasingly difficult to take a good deep breath. You probably make many more visits to the ladies' room than ever before. You may begin to suffer back pain as your body works to cope with all the extra weight you carry in front. If you have these symptoms, take heart. Most women experience at least some of them. Moreover, even less-frequent troubles like varicose veins or pregnancy-related diabetes usually don't last forever. The end is already in sight.

Perhaps your discomforts are so minor that you haven't given them much thought. You may take them as a matter of course—

a small price to pay for having a miracle unfold inside you. You may take them as nature's cue to start slowing down a little. Swollen ankles or varicose veins give you a pretty good hint that it's time to put your feet up and rest more often.

If your problems are more serious, though, you may worry both about your own health and that of your baby. If you've been plagued by nausea throughout your pregnancy, as some women are, you may worry that your baby may suffer. You may also wonder how much longer you can survive on soda crackers! If you had health problems before getting pregnant, you may have concerns about your body's ability to cope with the extra stress.

Even if you have no unusual problems, you may wonder if all that poking and prodding will damage your internal organs. Many women wonder at some point toward the end of their pregnancy if they're carrying twins: Can one baby take up so much space? Can all that poking and prodding really come from just one baby? In most cases it does. If you are carrying more than one baby, though, chances are that you are feeling increasingly uncomfortable—after all, there's a lot of baby in there!

Genesis gives a hint of how miserable such a pregnancy can be. Rebekah had been overjoyed to hear that she was pregnant. After all, she had been barren for so long that finally her husband took their fertility problems to the Lord in prayer. Getting pregnant wasn't the end of Rebekah's problems, however. Although she didn't yet know it, she was bearing twins. Those feisty twins stretched her belly. They pushed and shoved so much inside her that Rebekah felt like lying down to die: "If this is what it's like, why live?"

Can you relate to that? Rebekah had everything a woman in her day could desire—a good family with prospects for the future, a husband who loved her, and the pregnancy that she had longed for. Still, the suffering of the moment almost got the better of her. How easily troubles—whether they be physical aches and pains or psychological hurts and losses—push themselves onto center stage. God knows that and accepts our need to cry out in our pain. God didn't tell Rebekah to shut up and take her troubles like an adult. When Rebekah approached God with her troubles and asked why she should live, God helped her see the meaning in her suffering. God told her that she would give birth to two nations. Two sons already struggled in her womb; they would go on to become two nations. No wonder Rebekah suffered, with such a tussle going on inside her!

Most of us can endure a lot of suffering if we can see some meaning to it, and if we know it will come to an end. Even if you have severe aches and pains with your pregnancy, you know they will soon come to an end. As for meaning what could be more meaningful than bringing a child into the world?

Pregnancy stretches your womb. It can also stretch your soul. You find that you can cope with discomfort. You learn that you can give of your very self for the sake of another. You see that you can bring everything to God in prayer and that God will help you find the meaning and blessing in it.

Dear God, thank you for making me a person who can stretch. Help me learn and grow even from the aches and pains of pregnancy. Keep my baby healthy and strong. Help me rejoice in every one of its kicks! In Jesus' name, Amen.

✦ What meaning can you see in the discomfort of pregnancy?

"Then the dragon stood before the woman who was about to bear a child, so that he might devour her child as soon as it was born. And she gave birth to a son, a male child, who is to rule all the nations with a rod of iron. But her child was snatched away and taken to God and to his throne; and the woman fled into the wilderness, where she has a place prepared by God."
—Revelation 12:4–6

You probably will begin childbirth education classes soon, if you have not already done so. Check out the variety of prenatal courses available to you. Hospitals usually offer them. You may, however, prefer a course offered independently of the hospital. Childbirth education groups sponsor such courses in many communities. Some churches offer them as part of their ministry.

Look for a course that will give you well-rounded information on how your body functions and what to expect, tips on how to deal with labor, and a supportive, open environment. Ask class instructors how many sessions deal with preparation for labor. If this is your first baby, you will probably need five or six sessions on this topic. Ask new mothers if the class they attended gave them knowledge that they found helpful in their labors. Ask, too, if there was ample time for practicing relaxation and breathing exercises and for discussion and questions.

Once you have chosen a course, remember to enjoy it! You're not working to pass a test or to earn a diploma. You're absorbing and sifting through things that will help you make the best of whatever challenges your labor brings. You will learn many things: delightful things about how your body works and practical things like breathing techniques and how to position your pillows. You should learn how to get in tune with your body so your whole self will work together to do its birthing work.

You will probably make new friends and have a chance to share stories. You may get a charge out of listening to the wild dreams and weird cravings other women experience. Together you can chuckle over the practical drawbacks of big bellies: the shoelaces you can't tie, the positions you can't get into and the spots you can't get out of, the navel-gazing you can't do because your navel has disappeared.

You will also learn some upsetting things. You'll hear about back labor and episiotomies. You may see films of a cesarean birth as well as of a vaginal birth. The point of facing all kinds of unpleasant possibilities is to prepare you so you won't panic if your labor doesn't go smoothly. Try to take in this information without letting it overwhelm you; it will benefit you in the long run. The more you know about the birth process and obstetric procedures, the better you will be able to negotiate the kind of birth you want. Making an informed decision does often involve processing information that may be frightening: I sometimes almost wished the midwife wasn't so thorough in explaining the possible complications. Still, knowledge is power—and you will want a say in how your labor is managed.

In the meantime, don't focus too much on the scary possibilities. They are only possibilities; you may meet none of them. If you have to think about them, imagine yourself surviving them. Think of how you may react; plan strategies for rising to various challenges. If you find yourself focusing on some worst-case scenario, put things into perspective by reading the scary birth story John envisions in Revelations 12. He sees a beautifully clothed woman giving birth in the heavens. She struggles and cries out in her birth pangs, only to have a dragon appear just as she is about to give birth. Imagine giving birth with a dragon at your feet, ready to gobble up your child as soon as it is born! Makes any worst-case scenario you and I can cook up look like child's play.

The important thing to imprint upon your mind is that even a hungry dragon is no match for God. God saves both the woman and her newborn child from danger. The child is snatched away to safety as soon as it is born, and the woman flees to a wilderness hideout God had prepared for her. John's vision of birth in the heavens refers to a special birth with special dangers. It describes symbolically the Messiah's birth and the dangerous forces that try to prevent it.

Most babies don't put dragons on the defensive like the coming Messiah did. Still, every birth is a vulnerable time. You can't plan every detail in advance. You can't predict exactly what challenges will come up or control just how your labor will unfold. Still you are not powerless: you can learn as much as you can about the birthing process. You can make a practice of speaking openly to your doctor or midwife about your views on various treatments. You can plan to have your husband, or another trusted friend who knows your values, stand by your side during your labor. You can make all these preparations confident that God will help you rise to any challenge. In the midst of the wilderness God provides a safe haven. You and your baby are safe in the hands of the God who outwits and outmaneuvers even the scariest of dragons.

Dear God, thank you for my body and the wonderful things it can do. Thank you for my mind and all I am learning about how my body works. Give me the courage to ask questions and to voice my hopes and concerns. Give me flexibility and strength to face life's challenges. Help me find trustworthy helpers and trust you to help me through all danger. Amen.

✦ How are you preparing spiritually for the challenges of labor? What thoughts, images, and feelings have recurred most since you got pregnant? How do you see the Spirit leading you in these areas?

"So they picked Jonah up and threw him into the sea. . . .
But the Lord provided a large fish to swallow up Jonah;
and Jonah was in the belly of the fish three
days and three nights."
—Jonah 1:15-17

How do you feel about your ever-expanding belly? Maybe you watched with wonder and delight as your waist thickened and disappeared. Maybe you love pampering your growing body with lots of good food and exercise, and enjoy getting all the extra attention. On the other hand, your ballooning figure may get on your nerves. You wonder if it will ever stop swelling. Some days you feel sick of the whole thing: You wish you could maneuver as easily as before, snuggle into a comfortable sleeping position as easily as before, and pick things up as easily as before. You may resent your big belly, especially if you weren't planning to get pregnant. Even if you were eager to get pregnant, you may feel overwhelmed by your own body at times.

All of these feelings are normal. Take time to explore them and pray about them. There may be times when you feel like Jonah, wondering if you will be lost forever in a huge belly! I had days like that, especially the first time I was pregnant. Not only was my belly getting bigger and my energy level lower, but people seemed to focus more and more on my middle. This had its advantages, of course. I could usually count on a seat in the bus, even a crowded one. Strangers would strike up a conversation and give me a friendly pat on the belly. I usually enjoyed these cracks in the protective shell city dwellers build around themselves. Still, I sometimes felt lost in the role of "pregnant woman." At times it seemed as if the old me, with all her quirks and talents and interests, had been swallowed up by the belly I had become.

Take your belly experience as a chance to think, as Jonah did. For three long days and nights, Jonah sat in the belly of the fish and thought. He thought about the danger he'd been through. He thought about how foolish he had been to run away from the job God had called him to do. From inside that big belly, Jonah prayed. He poured out his fears to God. He gave thanks to God for saving him. He promised to face the challenges God set before him. With that, God spoke to the fish, and it spit Jonah back out onto the dry land. So, too, God will hear your prayers when you feel overwhelmed by your pregnancy and threatened by your changing shape. So, too, God will find ways to protect and care for you.

Maybe you feel you have more in common with the big fish than you do with Jonah. You may look at yourself in a mirror, and think, "I never dreamed I could get this big! I wonder if I'll ever get back to normal." The fish in the story is big—and important. The fish keeps Jonah safe in its big belly until it is time to spit him out. So, too, you protect and shelter the vulnerable little person who lives inside you. Your growing belly plays an important role in God's life-giving work. So glory in it! Think of it—your body can stretch and grow and make babies. Thank God for such a wonderful body and enjoy this time of being great with child!

The big fish didn't carry Jonah in its belly forever. Jonah stayed in there three days and nights, growing up in his faith. When the time was right, the fish listened to God and put Jonah back where he belonged. Similarly, when the time is right, God will work with you to bring your child out into the light of day. In the meantime, you have time to come to terms with your calling, as Jonah did in the belly of the fish. You have time to tune in to what God wants to say to you. You have time to tune in to your body and its many capabilities. You have time to stretch and grow in spirit. Before you know it, your body will give up its precious cargo and begin resuming a slimmer shape. Enjoy this time of blossoming. You are growing a new person!

Dear God, thank you for giving me a body that can do such marvelous things! My belly just keeps on stretching! Help me enjoy the changes rather than fight them. Forgive me if I'm sometimes down about the shape I'm in. I know you love me and will help me through all the ups and downs. Help me trust you. Help me trust my body. Help me learn from my body how to stretch my soul. Amen.

✦ Do people treat you differently now that you are visibly pregnant? How do you feel about that?

"The pangs of childbirth come for him, but he is an unwise son; for at the proper time he does not present himself at the mouth of the womb."
—Hosea 13:13

Do you know where your baby's head is? Perhaps your baby has already gotten into head down position. If so, he or she will probably stay that way. For one thing, there isn't much wiggle room left inside you. For another thing, right now the head is the biggest part of a baby's body; moving it against gravity's pull would take much effort. You and I would have a hard time standing on our heads for weeks at a time, but it seems to suit babies just fine. More important, it puts them in the perfect position for their head-first trip out into the light.

Most babies eventually get into the head-down position. When they do, their mothers can rest easier. If your baby does not move its head down within the next few weeks, your midwife or doctor may suggest exercises that encourage the baby to flip. If that fails, he or she may suggest trying to turn it from the outside. Some babies never do tip head down: they lay on their backs, or they sit upright. Either position makes it more difficult for them to make their way safely out through the birth canal.

Today if a vaginal birth doesn't work out because the baby is in an unfavorable position, you can still deliver a healthy baby by cesarean section. In the past, such a position could lead to the baby getting stuck in the birth canal. The prophet Hosea calls to mind just such a situation. Speaking on behalf of the Lord, he says Israel has behaved like an unwise son who does not come to the mouth of the womb at the proper time. This was not just a matter of coming late to an appointment. A prolonged and fruitless labor risked the lives of both child and mother.

Toward the end of my first pregnancy, I got a taste of how God must have felt about this. The joy of pregnancy was overshadowed when I learned that my baby was sitting tight with her head up. I faithfully tried all the exercises the midwife gave me. Several times a day, I got down on my forearms and knees, stuck my bottom way up in the air, and prayed for the baby to turn. I coaxed the baby to turn. I scolded the baby. I pleaded with the baby. I *willed* the baby to turn. No way. No headstands for this baby.

I prayed a lot in that awkward position. My elbows had calluses by the time I gave birth! I worried a lot, too. One worst-case scenario after the other pushed its way into my mind. In retrospect, I suspect that I was not only the concerned and frustrated mother, but also the unwise child. I couldn't seem to relax and let God help me through one way or another. Instead I almost choked on fruitless willing and pointless worries.

During these last few weeks of pregnancy, you too may meet obstacles—real or perceived. Sometimes even a childbirth educator's helpful attempts to forewarn you about things that *may* happen during childbirth wind up as grist for the worry mill. Share your concerns with your husband and trusted friends. They can help you sift the important concerns from the overblown ones. We don't always see the big picture, so it's good to have friends who see things through different eyes. Friends can give you emotional support, too, even if they can't completely understand the depth of your feelings. They can lift you and your concerns up in their prayers. We can't always lift our own spirits; sometimes we need to let the community of faith hold and lift us.

First and last, take your concerns to God in prayer. Ask God to strengthen you to cope with whatever real dangers come up. Ask God to help you face even your most irrational fears. Then let go of them, confident that God cares for you and your baby. God will help you both through the most trying of times. Let God help you learn to pray healthy, hopeful, trusting prayers now and in the weeks to come.

I never did manage to will that baby into turning. Still, she was brought out safely into the light—a healthy baby who has grown into a talented and delightful young woman. As for me, I survived the caesarean section I had so dreaded, and went on to deliver two more happy and healthy children without the surgeon's help. One way or another, God will help you through, too. You can count on it.

Dear God, help me trust you to take care of my baby and me. Help me trust my body to do its job. Strengthen my spirit to face whatever challenges come my way. Help me let go of foolish fears and bless the people who advise and care for me. In Jesus' name, Amen.

✦ What concerns you most about your pregnancy and the prospect of giving birth? What can you do about it?

*"I will fall upon them like a bear robbed of her cubs,
and will tear open the covering of their heart."
—Hosea 13:8*

*"As an eagle stirs up its nest, and hovers over its young;
as it spreads its wings, takes them up, and bears them aloft
on its pinions, the Lord alone guided him."
—Deuteronomy 32:11,12*

"Wouldn't you just kill for them?"

I stared in disbelief. This didn't sound like tender-hearted, fun-loving Laura.

"You never know how fierce you can be until you become a mother," she continued as she gently stroked the soft new skin of my baby's cheek.

Maybe you haven't felt such intense maternal passion yet, but don't be shocked if you do someday. Mothers have a reputation for strong protective instincts. Nobody wants to tangle with a mother bear. For that matter, think of the valor of a bird when someone gets too close to its nest: I once saw a red-winged blackbird make swooping attacks on a girl tens of times its own size. Human beings aren't quite like birds or bears, but parenthood still brings out very strong feelings.

Perhaps you have glimpsed some of these feelings in your dreams. You may dream that your baby gets hurt or lost. You may dream that you have to fend off strangers or wild animals. Find someone with whom you can share even your scariest dreams. This person might be a pregnant friend, your spiritual guide, your midwife, or your husband. Pregnant friends will probably nod in recognition and assure you that you are not the only one who dreams wild dreams. Your husband will have less firsthand experience of what you are going through, but he is in a position to comfort and support you when a bad dream awakens you. He may also help you interpret your dreams.

Your dreams can help you see the unruly emotions that you keep tucked away during the day. Dreams bring them to the surface and give you a chance to deal with them. None of us have nice, sweet feelings all the time. One woman dreamed that her baby cried so much that she finally threw it out the window. The dream helped her face the limits of her patience. It helped her admit that she might not always be able to handle her child's demands. She went on to be a fine, loving mother. Admitting her weakness was the first step toward achieving new strength and coping ability.

Perhaps your strongest current emotion is not fear or worry, but rather passionate attachment. You may have grown attached both to your baby and to the sheer wonder of being pregnant. You may be amazed to find your life revolving around your pregnancy. Perhaps you talk about little else. Perhaps you wonder why your husband doesn't show more interest. You may feel an increasing bond with all the pregnant women you see, smiling to one another and silently comparing the sizes of your bellies. Indeed, you may feel an almost mystical connection with mothers everywhere—and of all species. Whatever hardships pregnancy brings may fade in comparison with the primal experience of utter femaleness—ripe and brimming with life, immersed in one of life's deepest mysteries.

Not all women get caught up in such primal femaleness, of course. Even those who do experience such feelings may find them difficult to admit in a society that tries to minimize the differences between the sexes. No two women are quite the same, and even your own feelings may change a lot from day to day. Explore your feelings and your passions, whatever they may be. Bring them all to God—the scary ones as well as the beautiful ones. God will help you understand them and find ways to live fully with them.

Facing our fears and admitting our shortcomings is not an easy task. As the prophet Hosea warns, God has fierce maternal instincts, too: She is so protective of the best in her people that she tears away all that is self-destructive and bad. She tears open the hard, callous covering of our hearts. If that sounds scary and painful, remember that God's fierceness—like pregnancy itself—serves life. The ballet dancer Isadora Duncan had many emotional ups and downs while she was pregnant. She writes both of "the sanctity of the pregnant mother" and of how strange it felt to see her own "beautiful marble body softened and broken and stretched and deformed."

Pregnancy may soften and stretch marble bodies, but it also makes way for new horizons and new life. Facing our wildest fears and emotions may break down our old sense of self; it also makes way for a stronger and more realistic self to grow. The God who tears away our sinfulness is the same God who lovingly bears her young on her wings like a mother eagle. With God to correct and help us, we too can learn to fly.

Dear God, thank you for giving me feelings and a mind that tries to understand. Thank you for the many capabilities you have given me. Help me to face my fears and shortcomings. Help and guide me so that I grow stronger, more loving, and more courageous every day. Amen.

✦ How would you describe motherly love? What are its strengths? What are it weaknesses?

"This is my commandment, that you love one another as I have loved you. No one has greater love than this, to lay down one's life for one's friends."
—John 15:12 f.

When I lead women's retreats on the spiritual aspects of childbirth, I ask participants to reflect on the story of their own birth. I ask them to think about where they see God's hand in their story, and if their birth story has affected them later in life. The women share their stories in small groups, then we take time to sample a few with the group as a whole. The stories I hear are often dramatic: the baby's head emerges just as the doctor was going to get the forceps; labor lingers just long enough for the baby's father to arrive.

One grandmother told of her own birth many years ago. Labor had been long and difficult. Things looked so bad that the doctor recommended sacrificing the baby to save the mother's life. Hearing this out of a blur of pain and sedatives, the suffering mother cried out, "No! Dear God, save the baby!" Everyone returned to their work and their prayers with renewed effort, and both baby and mother survived to tell the tale. This woman always felt especially close to her mother. She knew that her mother's faith and courage had saved her life. Hearing this story brought out special feelings in this woman's friends, too. Suddenly the friend they had worked with and loved over the years seemed all the more precious; the world had almost missed the blessings she brought.

When someone we know has a brush with death, we get shaken out of taking that person for granted. We see in a flash how much that person means to us. So, too, a brush with death often makes people think more about their relationships and priorities. A prominent politician has a heart attack and then decides to leave the power and prestige of public life to spend more time with his family. A soldier in mortal combat experiences a fox-hole conversion.

In days gone by, childbirth, like soldiering, often included real danger of death. Thus in the early eighteenth century, the widely respected American preacher Cotton Mather vividly warned pregnant women that this might be their last chance to get right with the Lord. He saw pregnancy as a crucial time for women to get their spiritual house in order.

Facing death can give us a new outlook on life. If you thought today might be your last day, what would you do? Perhaps you would spend time in prayer; perhaps you would spend time talking with family and friends. Perhaps you would write a farewell love poem to your husband, like sixteenth-century poet Anne Bradstreet:

> *How soon, my Dear, death may my steps attend,*
> *How soon't may be thy lot to lose thy friend,*
> *We both are ignorant, yet love bids me*
> *These farewell lines to recommend thee . . .*

Bradstreet came safely through childbirth and lived to be sixty years old. Today there is very little risk that you might die in childbirth. Still, you may find yourself thinking about death more than usual. Many women do. Such thoughts are a natural response to being so intimately involved in the cycle of life. Psychologists Arthur and Libby Colman listened to many pregnant women. They observed that it seemed as if "by being closer to birth, to the beginning of life, these women were automatically closer to death." Pregnancy tends to put you in touch with your entire life cycle.

Indeed, giving birth may teach us much about dying—if we dare to think about it. In both cases human beings are humbled by the power of nature. We may be able to modify the natural processes of birth and death somewhat, but we can't completely control them. In both cases we rest our fates ultimately in God's hands. As Paul put it in Romans 14:8, "If we live, we live to the Lord, and if we die, we die to the Lord; so then, whether we live or whether we die, we are the Lord's."

Moreover, birth and death both mark transitions from one sphere to another. Thus a pregnant pastor developed a special bond with a woman dying of cancer: "We were both on the threshold of something radically new. We talked about that. When the baby was born, I sent her a picture, and she put in on her bedpost. A few days later she died. It was as if she had waited for the baby to be born."

Every moment of our lives is in God's hand, whether we stop to think about it or not. May pregnancy and childbirth stir up new appreciation of God's hand in your life. May the dangers of childbirth strip away the indifference that sometimes blinds us to the utter preciousness of life and love. Jesus showed how greatly he valued human lives and love when he laid down his life for us, that we might have life and have it abundantly. May Jesus' gift of life give you the faith and courage to lay down your life—and the grace to pick it up again and live it to the fullest.

Dear Jesus, you know I am frightened sometimes; help me face my fears and live through them. Thank you for facing death for us. Teach me to live every day as a precious gift from God. Help me appreciate my family and friends. Give me the faith and strength to love others as you have loved us.

✦ Has your pregnancy started you thinking about life and death more than you usually do? What new insights have you found?

8

Preparing for Birth Day

"On the eighth day they came to circumcise the child, and they were going to name him Zechariah after his father. But his mother said, 'No; he is to be called John.' They said to her, 'None of your relatives has this name.'"
—Luke 1:59-61

If you haven't already chosen a name for your child, you probably have at least begun to play with the possibilities. I loved poring over name books, learning what the names meant, and trying them out to hear how they would sound with our last name. Choosing a name can be such fun. The world is full of possibilities: Will this daughter be a Katherine or a Megan, an Amber or a Maria? Will this son be an Ilmar or an Eric, a David or a José?

Choosing a name is also a great responsibility. Johnny Cash used to sing a song about a "boy named Sue." The boy's father gave him a girl's name so that he would have to learn young to defend himself. The strategy worked; the poor boy got teased so much that he did indeed learn to be tough. Still, at the end of the song the boy who survived so much teasing counsels parents, "Never name a boy Sue!"

Few people go to such extremes when they name their children. Still, the name you choose for your child becomes an important part of his or her identity. Think about your own name. Did you have to stand up for it when you were a youngster? If you have an unusual name, you may have repeated its pronunciation or its spelling very often. My mother almost named me Solveig—a name that she associated with a lovely friend. She decided against the name because its Norwegian spelling and pronunciation might have burdened a little American girl. I sometimes wonder if I would have turned out any different if I had received that name.

Your name may connect you to other members of the family or the circumstances of your birth. My husband, for example, was named for the uncle on whose birthday he was born. A woman I know was named Faith after surviving a difficult birth. Your name may reflect your ethnic or religious background, or the popular culture of the years in which you were born. Recently I overheard a woman poking fun at her parents' choice of names for their children. "They didn't have much imagination. We all got the same names as half the kids in our class." I chuckled a few minutes later when I heard the same woman talking to her toddler son: "Come on Ryan, let's go!" A fine name, but hardly unique among boys his age!

When you choose a name for your child, you give him or her a lifelong gift. You want a name that will mean something special as well as a name that sounds good. Perhaps the name's meaning will lie in its family connections or its biblical or ethnic roots. Perhaps it will lie in the name's dictionary meaning. A friend welcomed our children into the world with plaques on which their names and their meanings were carved. Thus Sophia knows her name means wisdom; Niels knows his means champion; Anna knows hers means gracious.

Agreeing on a suitable name may take time, effort, and flexibility from both parents. A father comes with his family traditions and his preferences, just as a mother come with hers. Today, when many women keep their own family names, even figuring out a last name can take some doing! You want a name that you both like, a name that will serve your child well throughout a lifetime.

Sometimes parents can't make up their minds on a name until they see their baby. That may be what it takes to feel sure that the name really fits the person.

However long it takes, enjoy this opportunity to find a beautiful, meaningful name that will fit your child. Take it as an occasion for you and the baby's father to share stories of your own names as well as your ideas and hopes for your child. Pray together for guidance if you have trouble agreeing.

John the Baptist's parents prayed, too. For years they prayed that they might have children. When they finally did become parents, at least they didn't have to worry about finding a name for him. The angel who told Zechariah that his wife Elizabeth would soon bear a son also told him what to name the child. Zechariah and Elizabeth received a glimpse of their child's identity even before Elizabeth felt the baby stir in her womb. By the time the baby was born, there was no doubt in either of their minds that this new person was John—not Zechariah Jr. or Eli or Joshua, but John.

Few of us receive our child's name from an angel. An angel's command might remove the potential for conflict, but it would also remove the pleasure of making an important and joyous decision together. Take all the time you need. Listen to one another. Pray for wisdom and imagination, and trust the Spirit to help you make a good choice.

Dear God, thank you for giving us the child growing in my womb. Help us imagine what he or she will be like so we can find a name that will fit. Help us listen to each other and enjoy working together. Bless us as we choose our baby's name, and help us welcome this new person into our lives. In Jesus' name, Amen.

✦ What does your own name mean to you? What do you think is most important in choosing your baby's name?

"Like newborn infants, long for the pure spiritual milk, so that by it you may grow into salvation—if indeed you have tasted that the Lord is good."
—1 Peter 2:2 f.

Have you decided whether or not to breastfeed your child? Women throughout the ages have suckled their children. Other female mammals do so without giving it a thought. God has given you breasts that effortlessly make the perfect first food for your baby. Still, women debate whether or not to breastfeed. Some women wonder if they will have enough milk. Others wonder if nursing will harm their figure. One woman may wonder how to work breastfeeding into her public life; another may wonder if breastfeeding will make her husband feel jealous or left out.

Breastfeeding has gained in popularity in recent years. Perhaps you have friends or relatives who insist that breastfeeding is the only choice a true mother will make. Other friends argue that bottle-feeding is just as good and much more practical. How do you decide? If you are confused, you are not alone. We get many conflicting messages about our breasts from the society we live in. We hear that "breast is best"—a source of healthy, natural food with no artificial ingredients or wasteful packaging. On the other hand, female breasts are viewed as erotic objects; just glance through any girlie magazine. We get sentimental when we see pictures of a mother nursing her child—as long as the picture is set long ago and far away. If a modern mother reveals too much skin in nursing her child, people get uncomfortable.

Sifting through these mixed messages and deciding what is right for you may take some doing. Your success in breastfeeding depends largely upon how you *feel* about it. Most women are physically able to suckle their young successfully. If you want to do it, you probably can, especially if you receive support from your mate and others around you. If you or your husband have questions, read an informative book like Sheila Kitzinger's *The Experience of Breastfeeding.* If you cannot or do not want to breastfeed, don't feel guilty about it. The choice is yours—it's your body, your work schedule, your marriage, your feelings and values. Don't do it just because your mother tells you that it's your duty to suffer through it as she did for you.

For that matter, don't let anyone tell you that breastfeeding is a duty one suffers through, as one woman's mother did indeed tell her. I found breastfeeding utterly enjoyable, as well as very practical. No muss, no fuss, no mixing and heating. Instead the warmth of a little body snuggling close to your skin and the pleasure of a little mouth sucking at your breast, releasing the milk that has built up in your breasts. I wouldn't trade the experience for anything. You do need patience with yourself and with your baby. Nursing is not a test you can pass or fail. It may take a little time, but you will both get the hang of it.

A sense of humor helps. I remember waking some mornings feeling like I had two rocks on my chest because the baby had slept late and lots of milk had built up. I'd race downstairs, pick up two wide-mouthed teacups, and get busy. I must have made quite a picture, stripped to the waist, milk spurting out of both breasts into the cups placed strategically on the counter. I'd collect as much milk as possible before I heard a little voice cry. Then I'd quick transfer the milk to a bottle and put it in the freezer so mother's milk would always be available, even when mother wasn't.

Deciding whether or not to breastfeed is more than a matter of health and biology. It is also a spiritual issue. When you consider breastfeeding, you face your feelings about your God-given body. You explore whether you can accept and celebrate it—milk and all. You explore whether you can accept its limitations—the difficulties that you may meet and the practical awkwardness that sometimes comes up. You consider the relationships God has set you in: You think about your marriage. Breastfeeding may put a strain on it, or it may strengthen it as your husband supports you and appreciates your body in a new way. You think about your baby's health, and how you will respond to its little mouth at your breast. You may need to deal with feelings about your mother and her experience. You may need to deal with the practicalities of your work situation.

As you think about these things and make your decision, remember the apostle Peter's encouragement and advice: like newborn infants, long for Christ's pure spiritual milk. The risen Christ, who knows no bounds, will sense your longing and respond to your calls for help. A mother's milk begins to rush at the sound of her infant's cry, sometimes even at the mere thought of her child. Similarly, Christ's pure spiritual milk wells up at the sound of your voice. Christ overflows with delicious, nourishing goodness and wisdom. Drink it all in!

Dear God, thank you for giving me wonderful, productive breasts. Help me rejoice in my ability to make milk. Help me to enjoy the intimate contact of holding and feeding my baby whether I do it with a bottle or with my breast. Help me understand and respect my mate's feelings about breastfeeding. Help us grow together as we share decisions and responsibilities.

✦ What have you decided about breastfeeding? What does your decision tell you about yourself? Reflect on Peter's picture of Christ suckling human souls. How does this picture affect you?

"For you yourselves know very well that the day of the Lord will come like a thief in the night. When they say, 'There is peace and security,' then suddenly destruction will come upon them, as labor pains come upon a pregnant woman, and there will be no escape! But you, beloved, are not in darkness, for that day to surprise you like a thief; for you are all children of light and children of the day; we are not of the night or darkness."
—1 Thessalonians 5:2-5

"Be prepared." This motto from the Scouts serves equally well for the last few weeks of pregnancy. Months ago your doctor or midwife helped you figure out your "estimated date of delivery." Back then, the months of pregnancy probably seemed to loom endlessly ahead of you. Now that date will soon arrive. You may wonder if you will get all your preparations completed in time. Maybe you've begun making checklists: baby clothes, crib, and diapers; casseroles in the freezer; last projects at work; breathing techniques; tour of hospital; arrangements for older children . . . The lists could go on and on. You may also have parties and childbirth education classes to attend, not to mention increasingly frequent prenatal checkups. Sometimes your "due date" may feel like a deadline for getting everything ready.

Even if you have made most of your practical arrangements, you may wonder if you are emotionally and spiritually prepared for the challenges of childbirth. You may wonder how well your breathing and relaxation techniques will hold up when the going gets tough. If this is your first child, you may wonder how much labor will hurt and how you will take it. Perhaps you are eager to experience it all; perhaps you are a little afraid of the unknown. If you have given birth before, you may have mixed feelings based on how earlier births went.

Whatever your feelings, accept them and live through them. Face your fears and ask God to help you deal with them. Doing so will strengthen you, so you can rise to meet the challenges. Try to imagine the sources of strength that will help you through your labors, too: the people who will be on hand to help you; the God-given strength and capability of your body; the prayers of your friends, family, and fellow church members; the emotional strength you have built up dealing with other trying situations.

Prepare now—even if your "due date" is still weeks down the road. You are like a marathon runner preparing for a big race. You want both mind and body in peak condition for the stress and exhilaration of the trial ahead. So keep up your body: eat well, exercise, and get the rest you need. Nourish and exercise your spirit, too: learn as much as you can; share your concerns with someone you trust; envision strategies for dealing with difficulties; ask God to give you strength and peace, purpose and flexibility.

Running a marathon differs from giving birth in one important way. Runners usually know the exact date of the big race weeks and months in advance. You, on the other hand, know your *estimated* date of delivery, but no one knows exactly when your baby will make his or her big move. Your baby could come weeks early—or keep you waiting long days *after* your due date comes and goes. My husband and I arranged relatively free schedules around the expected arrival of our first child. We figured that Jørgen could safely resume preaching duties two weeks after my "due" date. So much for our reckoning—early that very Sunday morning I finally went into labor. If we'd known baby was waiting to add excitement to Sunday morning services, we could have signed up to preach a week earlier!

You do your best to make plans and continue living your life, all the while knowing that you may have to drop everything and rush to the birthing room. One woman told me that her waters broke a couple of weeks early, just as she took a big dinner out of the oven. Good-bye dinner party!

So, too, with our life as Christians. Christians, too, might well adopt the motto, "Be prepared." We don't know exactly when Christ will come again in glory, just as you don't know exactly when your birth pangs will start. We do know that we want to be prepared when Christ comes, just as you want to be prepared when labor starts turning your safe and tidy world upside down. Labor pangs are unavoidable; the baby has to get out somehow, and surgery is hardly less traumatic. Similarly, according to Paul, the transition from this world to the next will be traumatic, at least for those who roll through life in false security. On the other hand, those who know and love Christ are like well-prepared pregnant women. They face the birth pangs of the kingdom confident that a beautiful baby is on the way, and that God will help them meet every challenge and live through every trial.

Dear God, thank you for life in all its fullness and with all its surprises. Give me your peace as I wait for the first surprising signs of labor. Give me courage and strength as I face the unknown. Give me a thankful heart and help me share the love you have shown me in Jesus. Help me grow in grace and wisdom so that I will always be prepared for your kingdom to come. In Jesus' name, Amen.

✦ Do you feel physically and spiritually prepared for childbirth? Why or why not?

"So when you are offering your gift at the altar,
if you remember that your brother or sister has something
against you, leave your gift there before the altar and go;
first be reconciled to your brother or sister,
and then come and offer your gift."
—Matthew 5:23 f.

"Take a deep, cleansing breath," my childbirth educator used to say to the group assembled on the floor in front of her. Fifteen big bellies would move slightly as we all drew in as much air as we could, and then slowly blew the old spent air out again. The exercise cleaned out more than the air in our lungs. We breathed out the stresses and strains of the day. We began to relax and focus on the healthy rhythms of our bodies. Breathe in . . . breathe out . . . Slowly and deliberately, we let go of the garbage we'd been dragging around. Memories of aches and pains that had caused us to tense up began to fade. Muscles slowly relaxed. A sense of peace and simplicity washed over us.

Of all the breathing techniques I learned in prenatal classes, this is the one I remember—and still use. It helps me relax and get in tune with my body. It reminds me to expand my lungs and breathe in the fresh air. It reminds me to release hurts and bad feelings instead of letting them clog up my life.

These deep cleansing breaths help a lot during labor, too. Breathe out when you finish a contraction, and with that breath try to send out all the tension that has built up inside you. Exhale even the memory of the pain you just felt. Then focus on drawing in a slow, deep, cleansing breath. Open up and let the fresh new air rush in. It will invigorate and strengthen you to greet the next contraction. Start practicing now so that this breathing exercise is second nature by the time you give birth. It will help you relax and feel better now, too.

You may want to practice the classic Jesus prayer to the rhythms of your breathing: "Lord Jesus Christ, Son of God" as you slowly inhale; "Have mercy on me, a sinner" as you slowly exhale. When you do so, your physically and emotionally cleansing breath takes on spiritual dimensions, too. The longer I live, the more I realize that we all need daily forgiveness—for errors big and small; for the kind and courageous things we should have done and didn't; for the hurtful things we did do and wish we could undo. We need to forgive ourselves for our failings, and others for the hurts they have dished out to us. We need a regular cleansing breath to get rid of all the garbage that we accumulate in the course of our daily lives.

Jesus knew the healing power of forgiveness and reconciliation. He told his disciples to mend relationships with one another before they offer their gifts to God. Bad feelings, hurts, and wrongs tear a person apart; and a torn-apart person can't wholeheartedly offer thanks and praise to God. Similarly, a torn-apart person can't live a wholesome and full life. Studies show that people with lots of stress in their lives are more prone to illness. Maybe you know that from personal experience. I know that I don't sleep as well if I have troubles. I grind my teeth all night, and snap at my family the next day. Not exactly life in all its fullness!

Giving birth will call upon all of your resources. You want to be as healthy and whole as possible when you offer God the gift of your birthing labors. You want body and soul to work together, unhindered by bad feelings or stressful situations waiting in the wings. So take time to think about your relationships. Do some of them need mending? Ask for forgiveness if you have hurt someone. Pray for the strength and compassion to forgive those who have hurt you. If you need help, ask your pastor or a trusted Christian friend. Relationships are seldom mended overnight, but you can make a beginning. You can do your best to come to terms with the situation.

Think about your own sense of self, too. If for any reason you feel guilty or troubled, ask God to forgive you. Let the Holy Spirit blow a truly cleansing breath through your life. Let Jesus wash away all feelings of inadequacy or shame, resentment or cowardice, selfishness or carelessness. Ask God to forgive you, and ask God to help you forgive yourself. Then get on with life in all its fullness. Breathe in the fresh air of God's grace, and let God set free the happy, healthy, strong woman you are meant to be.

Dear Jesus, thank you for giving us the gift of forgiveness. Thank you for listening when I come with my troubles and cares and bad feelings. Thank you for giving me the courage and grace to try mending relationships that need it. Thank you for accepting me, encouraging me, and helping me to grow stronger and better every day. Amen.

✦ Where can you see a need for forgiveness and reconciliation in your life? What steps can you take toward healing?

"When she could hide him no longer she got a papyrus basket for him, and plastered it with bitumen and pitch; she put the child in it and placed it among the reeds on the bank of the river . . . The daughter of Pharaoh came down to bathe at the river, while her attendants walked beside the river. She saw the basket among the reeds and sent her maid to bring it. When she opened it, she saw the child. He was crying, and she took pity on him, 'This must be one of the Hebrew's children,' she said. Then his sister said to Pharaoh's daughter, 'Shall I go and get you a nurse from the Hebrew women to nurse the child for you?'"
—Exodus 2:3, 5 ff.

Have you talked with your midwife or doctor about a birth plan yet? Talking over such a plan gives you a chance to tell your caregiver how you feel about various procedures. If your caregiver knows your feelings and priorities, he or she will be better able to counsel and support you through your birthing. Similarly, if you know what the options and trade-offs are, you will feel more confident about making decisions.

My midwife took the initiative. She suggested that we compose a birth plan, write it all down, and put it on file in preparation for the big day. She had a whole checklist of things for me to think about: How do you feel about anesthetics? Episiotomy? Electronic fetal monitoring? Who will you want in the birthing room with you? What labor positions do you expect to use? Who do you want to cut the umbilical cord? Will you want the baby to room with you or go to the nursery?

If your doctor hasn't asked your preferences on such matters, take the initiative yourself. Think through your preferences and concerns, make a list, and at your next prenatal visit make a point of discussing it. Don't be shy! This is *your* birth experience, after all. If you feel nervous about suggesting things to a busy professional, take along your husband or a friend for moral support. You may need to negotiate some points with your doctor; you may want to revise or expand your list. When you feel satisfied with the list, make copies and ask your doctor to keep one ready on file. Give another copy to your husband, or whoever will be assisting you in the birthing room. Talk over your feelings with that person. That way he or she can help you respond to any unexpected challenges.

Such birth plans provide helpful guidelines; they aren't strict work orders. My midwife agreed to try to avoid an episiotomy by massaging my perineum with oil and helping me ease the baby's head out. Things didn't go quite that way. The umbilical cord had slipped down over my baby's head, so he didn't emerge fast enough. After a quick consultation, the midwife did an episiotomy (which I didn't even notice) that gave the baby just a little extra room. Out he popped—a beautiful, healthy little boy.

On the other hand, you may meet hospital rules that you can safely challenge. One hospital had a rule that limited women to a twenty-four hour "trial of labor" after their waters broke. If the baby wasn't born by that time, a cesarean section was required. None of my babies ever met that deadline; but thanks to the support and understanding of a wise obstetrician, I delivered vaginally in spite of the rules. She knew the medical literature and suggested that the risks involved in waiting another twenty-four hours were minimal for someone in my general health.

Making a birth plan helps you figure out your own values and express them. It encourages you to form plans and to find the flexibility to improvise on them. It challenges you to find a balance between your own desires and health, the health of your baby, and the habits of the health-care system. Fortunately, these three elements often coincide. You may question some medical interventions. You may wonder if some of the machines hinder more than they help. Still, most of us enjoy good medical care. We need not fear for our babies' survival, as women in some parts of the world do. We do not face evil plans like those that threatened baby Moses.

The story of Moses reminds us that even in the face of terrible threats, God works to strengthen and help people rise to the challenges they face. Moses' mother and Pharaoh's daughter didn't let the cruel, death-dealing commands of a powerful ruler go unchallenged. Moses' mother risked her life to hide him as long as she could and then let go of him in a daring plan that gave him a chance at life. Pharaoh's daughter risked her father's wrath by taking in a baby he viewed as the enemy. We don't even know the names of these women. Still, their story inspires us to keep our wits about us and to work against injustice wherever we meet it. Their story inspires us to use our minds and listen to our hearts, and to take risks in the service of life.

Dear God, thank you for giving me a mind able to make wise decisions and a heart full of compassion. Thank you for good health care and a stable society. Help me make wise plans for my baby's birth. Give me the courage to express my thoughts and desires. Give me the flexibility and wisdom to adjust plans if necessary. Give me faith in your unseen presence and support. In Jesus' name, Amen.

✦ What concerns and hopes do you have as you think ahead to giving birth?

"Rejoice always, pray without ceasing,
give thanks in all circumstances; for this is the
will of God in Christ Jesus for you."
—1 Thessalonians 5:16 ff.

"I can't believe it!" Our houseguest shook his head as he sat down to breakfast. "The mountains didn't catch my attention this morning when I opened the drapes. Every other morning they took my breath away. I guess I've been here too long."

How easily we miss the splendor of the life. Even snowcapped mountains looming in the distance can go unnoticed. Open your eyes, though, and sights as ordinary as a ladybug resting on a pale green stalk of grass can delight you. I walk our dog daily through a strip of vacant land under some power lines. When I open my senses, I can find beauty in either a cool refreshing drizzle or the soft glow of the evening sun. I can rejoice both in the vibrant blues, yellows, and whites of the wildflowers, and in the more subtle purple and red hues that crown the tall grasses. One day a warm breeze may bring me the scent of wild roses. Another day a brisk breeze may bring roses to my cheeks. Insects buzz and birds sing. I can open up and rejoice in the beauty and bounty around me—or I can walk right by it all, blinded by plans or worries.

I hope you remember to rejoice in the midst of all your plans and preparations. Pregnancy is such a special time—a time to rejoice in the miracle of life, a time to rejoice in simply being alive. Enjoy this time. Enjoy your special intimacy with your child—you will never be closer. For a few more weeks you will share the same body space, the same food, and the same air. Enjoy the simplicity of these days; you will soon have action and excitement to spare. For now, enjoy the freedom of going out without having to pack a diaper bag. Enjoy eating your meals in peace; enjoy providing perfectly for your baby with no muss or fuss. Rejoice in the miracle happening within you. Thank God for blessing you with a body that can make babies and a soul ready to love them.

Perhaps you find it hard to rejoice. We all have some bad days and some trying times. Some days you may be tired of the whole business—tired of feeling big and awkward, tired of waiting, tired of being tired. Perhaps your problems are more serious—your joy in pregnancy may have dimmed due to personal or health problems. You may have financial worries; your relationship with the baby's father may be rocky; prenatal screening may indicate potential health problems with your baby; sorrow or illness may cloud your path. Whatever your situation, the apostle Paul reminds you to rejoice always, pray ceaselessly, and give thanks in all circumstances.

If you take those words as a set of tasks to complete and standards to meet, they may sound overwhelming. How can you rejoice even when the world is caving in around your ears? How can any of us pray ceaselessly? None of us can live up to this high calling on our own. Paul reminds us, though, that we are not in this on our own. God wants us to live a life full of rejoicing, thankfulness, and prayer. Such a life is God's plan and will for us. Through Christ, God will help us to rejoice through thick and thin. God will help us make our very lives a prayer. God will help us see things to give thanks for in our darkest moments as well as in our happiest ones.

Paul's advice centers on prayer. When you pray, you open your heart and will to God—and you open your mind and senses to the world around you. Such an open heart finds cause for rejoicing in the little daily details of life as well as in the once-in-a-lifetime experiences. Such an open heart gives thanks for gifts high and low, in good times and in bad. The whole of our life can become a prayer of thanks and joy when we live it with God in mind.

Growing in faith and prayer doesn't shield us from the ups and downs of life. It does help us embrace and come to terms with all of life. A friend of mine told me once that she thought she might improve her prayer life by praying as she walked through some woods near her home. Everything went along fine until she realized that someone's dog had preceded her on her prayer hike. She had stepped right into the squishy smelly pile it had left behind! I think she stumbled onto a perfect picture of life on the prayer trail. Prayer isn't a romantic, otherworldly piece of froth. Jesus didn't lead us out of a messy world. Rather Jesus embraced life in all its complexity, with all its ups and all its downs. He showed us how to live life to the fullest—to laugh with those who laugh, and to weep with those who mourn.

So take Paul's words to heart. Rejoice and give thanks now in your pregnancy and in your preparations. Pray and prepare yourself to rejoice and give thanks in the midst of your birthing labors. Look forward to praying right through the first wild and woolly weeks with your newborn. God will help you rejoice and give thanks for everything—from a healthy load in your baby's diaper to a contented sucking at your breast!

Dear God, thank you for life; thank you for helping me to find new things to thank you for every day. Help me grow in my prayer life. Help me take in everything and present it to you. Help me rejoice in these last weeks of my pregnancy. Help me rejoice even when my birthing labors test my strength. Help me rejoice and give thanks for my baby and all the people I love. In Jesus' name, Amen.

✦ What are some of the wonders you have discovered during your pregnancy?

9

Living through Birthing Travail

"I will greatly increase your toil and your pregnancies; (Along) with travail shall you beget children. For to your man is your desire, And he shall predominate over you." —Genesis 3:16 (translated by Carol Meyers in Discovering Eve: Ancient Israelite Women in Context)

Pregnancy and childbirth do have elements of danger and distress. The Bible clearly regards childbearing as a blessing, but it does not minimize or ignore the suffering it involves. Genesis 3:16 sets out the trials and dangers we undergo on our way to the blessings of motherhood.

This basic honesty and realism is healthy. The more realistic your expectations about birthing distress, the better you will cope with it when the time comes. Canadian researchers found that Ukrainian Orthodox and Hutterite women experienced less pain in birthing than women from other cultural groups. These traditional Christian women expected some pain and saw it as a natural part of giving birth. They accepted their pangs as woman's share of the punishment for human sinfulness. This view apparently helped them through their birthing: They were seldom surprised by the intensity of labor and rarely requested pain medication. Many of their Anglo-Canadian counterparts had taken some form of childbirth education and hoped to have a drug-free birth. Still, they were often overwhelmed by labor and ended up asking for drugs to dull their pain.

We live in a culture that puts little premium on the ability to bear suffering. Even so, I would encourage you to prepare yourself to endure more distress than you think you can. Do this by learning to relax and pray. We make our own pain worse when we tense up in fear. The more you can learn to relax under stress and trust God to help you, the more easily labor will go. Do it by asking others for their prayers so you will know that you are not alone. Do it by getting your rest and exercise so your body will be in top form. Do it by remembering challenges you have lived up to in the past—the marathon you finished, the teeth straightening you survived, the hardship or loss you lived through.

Prepare yourself to outdo yourself in endurance for your baby's sake—the drugs that dull your sensations pass over the placenta into your baby's bloodstream, too. Do it for your own sake, too. Suffering is a part of life. When you choose to dull your pain, you dull your experience of life in all its variety. Moreover, you lose your chance to experience the euphoria that rushes in and washes away birthing distress. I know a woman who, while giving birth to her first child, felt she just couldn't handle any more pain. She asked her doctor for a spinal, and numbly delivered her baby half an hour later. She felt let down and strangely out of touch at the moment her baby was born. Afterward she told me that she wished she'd held out a little longer. She wished her doctor had told her that she was probably in transition, and that birth was probably close at hand.

You should of course take medication if you need it. Some labors are harder than others: Some babies get into difficult positions, and some are larger than their mother's pelvis can easily accommodate. This is a point at which you need to rely on good helpers. Let your doctor or midwife know in advance how you feel about pain medication so she or he can help you make good decisions in the midst of your labor pangs. Let your husband know how your feel, too, and encourage him to learn the signs that accompany transition. Transition is the hardest part of labor for many women—and it is a sign that means the job is almost done.

Childbirth is a challenge. It does involve blood, sweat, and tears. Yet, one woman admitted bashfully that her labor was no more painful than passing an unusually large bowel movement. Most English translations of the Bible do us a disservice by reading pain into Genesis 3:16. The English word "toil" is much closer to the Hebrew original—and much closer to the way women experience an uncomplicated birth. Your birthing body works very hard. Some muscles tighten and press down on others with great force. Tiny openings stretch enough to let a whole baby get through. All that hard work does hurt some, of course. It would be foolish to pretend it didn't. Your uterus is the strongest muscle in your body—when it flexes and shows its power, you notice!

However challenging your labor turns out to be, take your birth pangs as a sign of your body's strength and a chance to try your spirit's ability to endure. Take them as an opportunity to experience life—agony as well as ecstasy. Take them as a sign of the worthwhile work you are doing. How many important things get accomplished without a struggle? Take them as a challenging adventure on the road to motherhood.

Dear God, thank you for my body. Help me accept and enjoy its show of strength in labor. Help me when suffering tests my limits. Assure me that you will not let me suffer more than I can bear, and that you will always be with me. Amen.

✦ How do you view the discomfort and pain of childbirth?

"Unto the woman [the Lord God] said,
'I will greatly multiply your toil in pregnancy;
in grievous toil you will bear children' . . . And to the
man he said . . . 'cursed is the ground because of you;
in toil you shall eat of it all the days of your life.'"
—Genesis 3:16,17 (author's translation)

Toil, toil, grievous toil—what does it mean? Toil is hard physical labor made worse by a burden of worry and fear. Toil means more than aching muscles; it also means an aching soul. Adam and Eve called the grief and distress of toil down upon themselves. To a great extent that distress is an unfortunate side effect of eating the forbidden fruit. Eating that tempting morsel did open their eyes, as the serpent had promised. No longer were they innocent children. Suddenly they could see themselves as others saw them. They could see that they were naked and reached for the fig leaves. They could begin to see what the future might bring. They could begin to imagine that things might go wrong. The toil of childbirth is more than the hurt, stress, and strain of hardworking muscles. It is labor made harder by fear, tension, and worry.

We can't roll back the story and go back to a state of inexperienced innocence. We can, however, live through our distressing toil—and the story gives us several hints on how to do this.

First, the story reminds us that we are in this together. Adam's and Eve's punishments are linked. The very vocabulary of the original Hebrew shows this. The word *toil* comes up three times, as you can see in the verses quoted above. Moreover, man and woman share in each other's punishments. Over the centuries women have shared in the toil of putting bread and butter on the table. And, as church reformer Martin Luther observed almost 500 years ago, part of woman's punishment is transferred to her husband, "for he cannot without grief" see his wife suffer in childbirth. A man suffers as he stands by helplessly while his loved one travails, but his very presence encourages and strengthens her for her labors.

Second, the story shows God standing by Adam and Eve in spite of their disobedience. God doesn't just walk away and let the forbidden fruit take its unhappy toll. Like a good parent, God talks to Adam and Eve and helps them see what they did wrong. Then God punishes them. Few of us like to be punished. Still, punishment is a sign of respect. We punish our children when they misbehave because we love them and want them to learn good and healthy ways. We punish them because we respect them and think they are capable of learning right from wrong. So, too, God respects Adam and Eve enough to punish them.

This is particularly important for women. In many times and places, women have been viewed as legal and moral incompetents. Genesis shows us that God respects women as well as men. God holds each of us accountable for our actions. Childbirth is a point at which we women seem most governed by our bodies; yet it is precisely here that Genesis reminds us of our spiritual nature and our relationship to God. Our birthing woes become a reminder that God respects us and regards us as capable and responsible people.

Finally, the story prods us to look into our own lives. You may think it unfair that all women are punished for Eve's disobedience—and yet who lives a life of perfect trust in our Creator? Increased trust in your Creator and in your Creator's handiwork will not erase your birth pangs entirely. Eve's toil was increased, after all, not introduced. Still, the more you trust God to help you, the more your body will be freed to do its best. Eve came through her travail with words of wonder and fulfillment on her lips. I hope you can do the same!

Dear God, help me see my birth pangs in light of the big picture of your love and respect for all creation. Thank you for standing by us, even when we let you down. Thank you for giving us one another, so we can share our burdens and our joys. Thank you for respecting me and caring for me. Help me trust you more each day. Amen.

✦ How does your faith help you face childbirth?

"Yet she will be saved through childbearing, provided they continue in faith and love and holiness, with modesty."
—1 Timothy 2:15

"Christian women don't need to suffer in childbirth. Childbirth pain was punishment for Eve's sin; now Jesus has paid for all our sins," Melanie said. She rose slowly from her gardening and brushed some soil off her hands. She put her hands where her waist had been and stretched her back. Soon she would give birth to her third child.

There may have been a bit of wishful thinking in Melanie's theology. Her first two children had been born before she became a Christian. Still, she had a point. Jesus did more than teach and preach. He forgave sins and brought healing to suffering people. Christianity is more than pie in the sky.

The New Testament letter of First Timothy contains a promise that woman will be preserved through the dangers of childbirth. The promise is clumsily worded; perhaps that is why it has often been taken to mean that women will be saved by virtue of giving birth. That reading does not agree with the rest of the Bible, however. As Melanie said, Jesus has already paid for our sins. We don't have to give birth or do good deeds in order to be saved. Jesus has already done the hard work for us and offers us life and salvation as a gift.

Even so, faithful Christian women sometimes face difficult labors. God doesn't promise us a life without suffering, but Jesus will help us live through and beyond whatever suffering comes our way. Saint Paul proclaims that nothing can separate us from the love of God in Christ Jesus—neither death nor life, neither things present nor things to come, nor anything in all creation. Hang on to that promise! It will help you face anything with courage and peace.

Think about your faith and its symbols as you prepare for the day you give birth. If you plan to give birth in a hospital or birthing center, you may already have packed personal items to take with you. If you are preparing to give birth at home, you may have collected the bedding and other things you will need. Take time to include items that will remind you of your faith. Perhaps you will want to focus on a cross or crucifix, or a favorite picture of the Madonna and Child. Such symbols can help you see through your suffering to the larger picture of Christ's work in the world. You may want to light a candle to remind you of the light of Christ—the light that the darkness has never overcome. You may enjoy tapes of Christian music. Look for songs and hymns of gentle assurance for your labor, as well as more vigorous, joyful hymns and choruses for later when you push and then celebrate.

Reminders of your faith can help you see your birthing labors in a holy light. They may also bear witness to your birth attendants. A doctor described the spiritual impact of a birth she once attended. Throughout labor, the couple played spirituals and gospel songs softly in the background. The husband held his wife's hand and prayed out loud at times, he massaged her back and sang softly at other times. Labor went extraordinarily smoothly; the bag of waters cushioned the baby until it emerged from the womb. The doctor summed things up by saying, "I felt like we had touched the center of peace on earth."

Giving birth can be happy and holy, even if it doesn't go quite so smoothly. Even if you don't manage to take a single prop along with you, God has given you spiritual gifts that can see you through your labors. The first book of Timothy notes several of these gifts: faith, love, holiness, and modesty. You can probably see how faith and love will help you: Your faith will give you confidence and courage. Love gives your labors their purpose.

You may wonder, though, how holiness fits in. Perhaps you don't think of yourself as holy. Still, God gives you holiness as a gift. In your baptism, you were set apart for God; you were marked with the cross of Christ forever. And with God's help you grow in grace and holiness throughout your life. As you grow in holiness you become a more whole person: Holiness draws all of life's ups and downs into a grace-filled whole. The agony and the ecstasy of giving birth will give you plenty of opportunity to taste that wholeness. You offer your whole self up to God's creative purposes. You receive the satisfaction of doing life-giving, holy work.

Finally, 1 Timothy mentions modesty. Don't worry; the Bible is not telling you to keep yourself covered at all costs! The Greek word translated above as "modesty" means more than not flaunting your body or your abilities. It could also be translated as good sense or self-discipline. You probably won't feel tempted to flaunt your body in the midst of giving birth; you will have more important things to do. And that is where the spiritual gift of modesty and self-discipline comes in. This spiritual gift means making sound and disciplined use of all your abilities so that you can do good and important things. Modesty means that you do things rather than showing off or boasting. Self-discipline means that you keep your spiritual balance—the balance that will help you stay afloat through even the stormiest labor.

Christian women may not avoid pain when they give birth, but they have received the spiritual gifts to help them live and rejoice through it all. Faith, love, and holiness with self-discipline can transform even the hardest birthing labors into a disciplined, creative, and joyous prayer.

Dear God, thank you for standing by me always, even when I can't see you. Thank you for Jesus' offer of life and wholeness. Help me believe your promises each day. Help me sense your presence with me now and when I give birth. Amen.

✦ Who or what do you trust to help you through your birthing work?

"And going a little farther, he threw himself on the ground and prayed that, if it were possible, the hour might pass from him. He said 'Abba, Father, for you all things are possible; remove this cup from me; yet, not what I want, but what you want.'"
—Mark 14:35 f.

"I gave birth before natural childbirth came into fashion," Irene said, "so I don't remember much about the birth itself. One thing I do remember, though: I did not want to go to the hospital!"

How will you feel when the big day arrives? Maybe you will rush to the hospital in excitement. Perhaps you will drag your feet. Like Irene, you may realize that deep down inside you don't want to go to the hospital.

Perhaps you can relate to both sets of feelings. You may be growing more and more eager to see and touch your baby.

If this is your first child, you may especially look forward to experiencing birth for yourself. After all you have learned about childbirth, you may look forward to seeing what your body can do. At the same time, you may wish you could have your baby without going through the pain and uncertainty of labor. You may get flashes of stage fright and worry that you will forget all the breathing and relaxation techniques you have been practicing.

Mixed feelings are perfectly normal. You face an unfamiliar test of your physical and spiritual strength. After all, few women in today's western world ever become old hands at giving birth. If you have given birth before, you know just how challenging labor can be. Moreover, every labor presents its own mix of challenges and joys. Your whole being is called upon to open up and do the important work of pushing a vulnerable little being out of one realm and into another. Most of us wonder how it will go and how we will respond under pressure.

Accept your mixed feelings, and then put them in your Creator's hands. Even if you do forget every breathing technique you ever learned, God has given you a body that knows what to do. Most women could probably deliver their babies all alone if necessary.

Few of us do deliver our babies alone. Most of us choose to give birth in a hospital or birthing center, surrounded by helpful professionals and with ready access to the latest medical technology. Why, then, do some women want to put off the trip to the hospital? I think that it is more than fear of impending pain. Irene gave birth while heavily sedated, and she still hated going to the hospital.

Perhaps Irene dreaded the impersonality of the hospital and the foreignness of its routines. Touring your hospital's maternity ward in advance may minimize that problem, although it probably will not eliminate it. When you enter the hospital in labor, staff people treat you as a patient. You sign in and get a patient number. You take off your own clothes and put on a hospital gown. You may feel that you lose control over your own situation. Suddenly strangers take charge of when and if you can eat. They may hook you up to machines you don't completely understand. They come in and out of your room at will.

Giving birth does involve losing some of the control we take for granted. Even the most relaxed hospital atmosphere and sensitive, helpful staff cannot change that. Your body is going to do its thing whether you like it or not. When your contractions are well under way, there is no turning back. You can work with your body or you can fight it, but you can't stop what your body has set in motion. You are borne along by the powerful forces of nature.

That may sound a little scary. You may wish you could opt out at the last minute. You may find yourself echoing Jesus' prayer in the garden of Gethsemane: dear God, for you all things are possible, remove this cup from me. Jesus knew he was headed for suffering. He didn't want to suffer any more than you do, but he didn't run away from suffering either. Instead he put his fate in God's hands: "remove this cup from me; yet, not what I want, but what you want."

God helped Jesus live through his fate. So, too, God will help you live through yours. Like Jesus, find freedom and courage by putting yourself in God's hands. Trust God; trust the body God has given you; trust the helpers God has provided for you. Then let yourself go, confident that God will guide you through the unknown and help you rise to every challenge.

Dear God, you know that I am scared sometimes. Help me trust you and my body. Help me find trustworthy helpers, and help me to trust them. Help me welcome the surge of nature's power moving through me to bring forth my baby. Give me courage to face the unknown; give me the strength to bear whatever hardships life brings my way. In Jesus' name, Amen.

✦ How do you feel about the prospect of losing some of your usual control over your body during childbirth?

"Labor and bring forth, O daughter Zion,
like a woman giving birth; for now you shall go forth
from the city and camp in the open country; you shall go
to Babylon. There you shall be rescued, there the Lord
will redeem you from the hand of your enemies."
—Micah 4:10 (translation amended by author)

Annie was surprised at the powerful rush she got from the strong forces birthing unleashed within her. She said later that she had felt like swinging from the chandelier. Elisabeth was shocked at the nasty remarks she had made to her husband. "I don't usually talk that way," she said apologetically afterward.

Birthing brings surprises to many of us, even if we know generally how the process goes. You never know just how you will react. We've all heard stories of the woman who lashes out at her husband for getting her into such a fix. Some women feel like forgetting the whole thing and going home—right in the middle of it all. You may keep quiet; you may groan and shout. You may want your husband to leave you alone one minute and insist that he stay by your side the next.

You need to feel free to let loose. Discuss this in advance with your husband or whomever you plan to have with you during labor. Your companion needs to know that whatever rude remarks come flying out should be taken with a large grain of salt. You will feel more free to do whatever you need to do if you have forewarned your helper. Moreover, he or she can help you a lot by encouraging you to let loose and let go. One midwife observed that when a birthing woman finally lets go of all her inhibitions, birth usually comes very quickly.

How intricately the human body and soul are knit together! Your body will squeeze and push until the baby comes out, whether you like it or not. But if you let go and get into the flow of your contractions, your mind and soul will help your body make it a grace-filled experience. Body and soul will work together to bring about a joyous result.

Letting yourself go like this takes some shifting of gears. You probably have trained your mind and soul to control what your body does. Childbirth turns all that upside down. Even toilet training slips away for a time. You just cannot resist your body's urges. Your body takes the reins, and all you can do is ask mind and soul to let go of them graciously. That takes courage. You need to trust your body and your helpers. You need to trust God to help you pull yourself together again.

Letting go takes courage, but it also brings freedom. You can immerse yourself in the task at hand, rather than resisting the distressing symptoms. The ability to let go and trust God to help you face difficulties will serve you well throughout your life. "Labor and bring forth," the prophet Micah encouraged God's people as they faced deportation to Babylon. The people could see bad times coming. They didn't know what would happen to them. They felt scared and unable to control their own future. Micah encouraged them to take their troubles as birth pangs—a beginning rather than an end. "Get on with it," he seems to say. "Put your energies into the life-giving work of your contractions and bring forth the baby you carry within you. No matter how long you spend in the wilderness of travail, know that God will help you. God will deliver you in the end."

Unfortunately, translations generally muddle Micah's words of encouragement. The common translation, "writhe and groan," reads pain into the process. Micah's words do the opposite. Micah takes bad times as a starting point; then he reads hope into the situation by rephrasing in terms of birth. The word commonly translated "writhe" refers to having labor contractions. The word translated "groan" refers to pushing the baby out into the world. "Labor and bring forth" is a more accurate and helpful translation.

There may be times in your labor when you, too, feel scared and out of control. There may be times when labor seems to stretch out like an endless wilderness. There may be times when you feel like giving up. I told my husband at one point during my first vaginal birth that I didn't think I'd be able to go much longer without some kind of help. He looked at me and said, "What do you mean? I thought this was what you wanted!" I was irritated with him at the time, but I thanked him later. In his own way he was delivering Micah's message: "Don't hold back or give up now. Labor and bring forth!" Within half an hour the baby was born.

Take your labor as a chance to learn to let go. Take the chance to immerse yourself in a wondrous labor of love, confident in your body's powers and in God's help. "Work with your contractions and bring forth!"

Dear God, thank you for protecting and caring for my baby and me. Keep us safe through whatever challenges labor brings. Help me trust you and my body so I can loosen up instead of trying to stay in control. Give my labor companion a forgiving spirit, in case I say rude things. Give him or her wisdom, in case I need fresh insight.

✦ How do you think your spirit will affect your body's birthing work?

"But God raised [Jesus] up, having loosed the birth pangs of death, because it was not possible for him to be held by it."
—Acts 2:24 (author's translation)

"I never understood the crucifixion until I gave birth," Carolyn said. Bible study members shifted uncomfortably in their seats. "Was labor really that bad?" asked Marty.

Comparing childbirth to crucifixion may sound grotesque and scary. I remember being shocked by medieval visions of Christ giving birth on the cross and suckling faithful souls with his own blood. The monks and nuns who recorded such insights had not given birth themselves; obviously they were not trying to describe the ordeal of childbirth. Rather, they were stretching to find a picture from daily life that could give insight into Jesus' life-giving suffering.

Centuries later, Carolyn did the same thing. She gained insight into Jesus' suffering on the cross by thinking about her own experience of giving birth. "No, my labor wasn't bad at all," she answered Marty. "I know Jesus' sufferings on the cross were much worse than anything I went through. But I think I got a taste of how he must have felt—knowing he had to finish what he'd begun. There's no easy way out when you're giving birth, either. Like it or not, you have to go through some suffering. It's suffering with a purpose, though. You suffer to bring forth life. That's what Jesus did, too."

The more I think about the picture of Jesus giving birth on the cross, the more helpful I find it. Think of it: Jesus has gone through birthing labors much worse than you will have to endure. Jesus endured the worst-case birthing scenario: the birth pangs of death. Happily for us, that is not the end of the story. As Peter points out in Acts, God raised Christ up. The birth pangs of death could not hold our brave, holy mother.

When you go into labor, remember that Christ leads the way. You may want to modify the classic Jesus breathing prayer to draw strength from picturing Christ as your mother and sister. Breath in calling on "Lord Jesus Christ, who gave birth on the cross." Breathe out praying, "Bless me as I labor." This prayer puts your birthing struggles into Christian perspective. It can give you peace and purpose during the first stages of labor. Don't worry if you can't keep up the whole prayer all the way through labor. The Spirit flutters over us and helps us, praying for us with groans too deep for words.

Very few women today come anywhere near the worst-case scenario Jesus experienced. Even so, you may find that the possibility of death crosses your mind and enters into your dreams more often than usual. Don't let such thoughts trouble you; they often accompany pregnancy. There are good reasons for these thoughts, even if actual death is only an extremely remote possibility. You do bear a precious treasure within you. You do face some risks in labor. Your child's birth will bring you new responsibilities and an important new reason to live. Moreover, you will go through a kind of dying and rising, even if you and your baby have a perfectly safe and normal birth. You will go into the hospital as a pregnant woman and emerge days or hours later as a postpartum one.

Perhaps you have already begun to grieve for your pregnant self. You may feel inexplicably sad some days and wonder why, now that the day you have been awaiting finally draws near. These feelings don't mean that you love your baby any less or that you are an emotional basket case. It took some doing to get used to the rich and fertile pregnant version of yourself and all the attention it brings. It may also take some doing to let go of that pregnant self. Feel free to mourn the passing of this brief but wondrous time in your life.

Find ways to celebrate this special chapter in your life, too. Take time to make a "great with child" list: note all the surprises and delights of your pregnancy. Read through your journal, if you have been keeping one. Recall the funny feelings and incidents; think about the ups and downs and how you pulled through them. Thank God for the people who have helped and encouraged you: the older woman who always asked how you were feeling; your husband, who did everything from tying your shoes to giving you moral support; the neighbor boy who helped you get your groceries into the kitchen.

Start saying good-bye to your pregnant self, and prepare to say hello to the new self who will emerge on the other side of childbirth. God raised Jesus up from his birthing travail, and God will raise you up, too. God has brought you safely thus far, and God will help you through your birth pangs. God will help you rise to the challenges of motherhood and whatever the future may bring.

Dear Jesus, thank you for helping me through all my ups and downs. Help me remember you when I give birth. Give me courage and strength to do what needs to be done, just as you did. Thank you for sharing our struggles and sorrows, and for giving birth to new hope and life on the cross. Amen.

✦ What do you think of interpreting the crucifixion as Jesus giving birth to a new creation? Can you see Christ as your mother and sister? How might this picture help you through childbirth?

"When a woman is giving birth, she has sorrow, because her hour has come; but when she has borne the child, she no longer remembers the distress, for joy that a human being has been born into the world. So you will have sorrow now, but I will see you again, and your hearts will rejoice, and no one will take your joy from you."
—John 16:2 f. (author's translation)

I expected the birth of our third child to go smoothly. Labor had gone surprisingly quickly and easily the last time around. I felt calmer and more relaxed than I had while awaiting the births of either of our first two children. Perhaps I had relaxed a little too much: days went by after my waters broke and there were still no contractions! On the third morning we decided to induce labor. I believed that we had made a wise decision; even so I was really down in the dumps when the nurse came in to hook me up to the IV tubes and start the pitocin drip.

As time went on, I also found the contractions harder to take than those I remembered from my previous labor. By that evening I could no longer get out of bed to walk around, so I felt sure that I must be getting close to delivery. Ruth, my midwife, checked to see how far I had dilated and reported that there were still several centimeters left to go. Did I ever feel discouraged! Labor didn't last long after that low point though. An hour later I was pushing baby out into the world.

As Jesus said in the comforting parable quoted above, you do tend to forget whatever distress you endured in order to give birth. For many women, joy swallows up all sorrow the very moment they deliver their child. Some women describe the feeling of pushing their baby out into the world as a rush, a true high. Some laugh through tears of joy. Many instinctively begin to comfort their newborn—cooing "it's all right" as they pat and stroke the new little wonder.

You, too, may need extra comfort and care in the moments following the exertions of birth, especially if the birth was difficult. After the hubbub of pushing baby number three out into the world had subsided, my midwife offered to pray with us. Our newborn rested on my abdomen while Jørgen, Ruth, and Serena gathered around us. Serena was new to Jørgen and me. She had come from out of town to visit Ruth, and ended up spending the day in the hospital tea kitchen. Unknown to us, she felt a part of our baby's birth, too. We all joined hands and Ruth led us in prayer. She thanked God for a safe birth and asked God to heal whatever hurts or painful memories baby or I might have. The prayer surrounded us with blessing and peace at the end of an eventful day.

I hope that someday such a prayer will become a regular part of birth. Ruth had served many years as a medical missionary, so this came naturally to her. Praying with you may not come as naturally to your doctor or midwife. Few medical schools include the use of prayer in their training programs. Even so, your midwife or doctor might be willing to lead a prayer of thanks following birth, especially if you ask in advance. Otherwise you might ask your husband or labor companion to help in this way. The simplest prayer can mean a lot on such an occasion.

My joy at my children's births didn't wipe out the memory of the struggles I had gone through. Ruth's prayer didn't erase those memories either. The joy and the prayer did help to heal and transform my memories into priceless treasures. I wouldn't want to forget a single minute of my labors, even if I could. I keep them all stored in my heart—the ups and downs, the moments of discouragement and the moments of grace, the exhilaration, the struggle, and the release I felt as I labored to bring a new human being into the world.

I store those memories in my heart and draw strength from them. When I feel myself tensing up in the dentist's chair, I think to myself, "Relax, this is nothing compared to what you've been through." When I face a difficult meeting, I breathe my birthing prayer: "Lord Jesus Christ, who gave birth on the cross; bless me in my labor."

Jesus, too, drew on the experience of birthing women to comfort and strengthen his followers. "See your trials and hardships in the light of childbirth," he encouraged them. Women live through their birthing travail and forget its distress in the overwhelming joy of birth. So, too, you can face trials of every sort, knowing that joy awaits you. You can do it: With God's help you can do it, no matter how bleak things sometimes look.

Jesus' promise extends to us, too. We can endure hardships or trials because we know that joy awaits us. We can live faithful lives confident that when our earthly labors come to an end we too will see Christ. Finally, just as birthing travail gives way to wondrous joy, so too all our sorrows will give way to unending joy.

Dear God, thank you for watching over me while I labor. Thank you for the prayers of your people and for the joy that will soon be mine. Help me see your hand at work in my life. Help me draw strength from my struggles and rejoice in the life you have given me. In Jesus' name, Amen.

✦ How do you feel about losing your pregnant self? What insights have you gained during your pregnancy?

10

After Birth

"Hannah prayed and said, 'My heart exults in the Lord; my strength is exalted in my God. My mouth derides my enemies, because I rejoice in my victory.'"
—1 Samuel 2:1

Congratulations! You did it! Your labor may have rolled along quickly and easily, or you may have worked long and hard. You may have managed without any medical procedures, or you may have delivered your baby by cesarean section. However you did it, glory in it! You put your life on the line and brought forth your baby! As one grandmother said when she thought back on her first child's birth, "I felt like shouting from the housetops! It was really something to crow about."

You do have plenty to crow about: What a wonderful piece of work you and God have accomplished! By this time you and your husband have probably examined your baby from head to foot. You have probably counted all the perfect little fingers and toes, and perhaps wondered at the miniature fingernails. You've had a chance to look into your baby's wide eyes, and you've had a chance to admire his or her delicate eyelids with their fringe of fine eyelashes. Your baby may be so tiny that it will spend its first days in an incubator. Or it may be so large that you can scarcely believe that you could open wide enough to let it get out. Your baby may have emerged in perfect form, or its journey through the birth canal may have pressed its head temporarily out of shape.

Whatever your baby looks like, he or she is a magnificent piece of work! Each and every baby is a wonderful addition to the human race. On behalf of the rest of us, let me thank you! Thank you for the hard work and strain of birthing your baby. Thank you for the energy you put into your pregnancy—your attention to diet and exercise, your prayers and your endurance of discomforts, your willingness to put your health on the line, and the spiritual energy you put into preparing for your baby. Thanks in advance for all the love, care, and guidance you and your mate will give your baby as the years go by. Thank you for your part in making a miracle!

Your baby is a miracle! You probably agree wholeheartedly and don't need a word of convincing. God makes quite an impression when a child comes into the world. Even parents who have little time for religion readily agree that their child is a miracle. We stand in awe, regardless of how much or how little we think about God in our daily lives. The sixteenth-century church reformer Martin Luther lifted up this widespread miracle and encouraged people to honor it. He thought it a good idea that people "kiss the newborn infant, even before it is baptized, in honor of the hands of God here engaged in a brand new deed." That's high praise indeed coming from a church leader who cherished the gift of infant baptism, and who lived in a time when many viewed unbaptized babies as unclean.

Glory in this miracle God has worked in and with you! Celebrate God's work and celebrate your own strength. Celebrate having played such a central role in a miracle. You are not just an "extra" in the drama of your child's life. You and your husband play leading roles, and you have God to help you. Now that's something to celebrate!

The biblical Hannah knew she had something to celebrate, and she sang a victory song: "My heart exults in the Lord, my strength is exalted in my God." With God's help, you too emerged victorious from whatever dangers you faced in childbirth. So exult as Hannah did! With God's help, your strength, too, will carry you through the long haul. Hannah sings such an inspiring song. In one breath she glories in God, who helped her through her difficulties. In the next breath she crows with pride in her own God-given strength. You get the feeling that God also glories in the happy outcome of their joint venture.

Hannah saw her victory as a gift of God. She freely admits that she couldn't have done it without God—but that doesn't make her think any less of her own strength and capabilities. Rather she felt great because God had helped her bring forth a miracle. She knew that she had offered her strength and her prayers in a life-giving effort far greater than she herself. You are in the same position, so take a cue from Hannah, and celebrate your strength! Celebrate God's handiwork in your life! Celebrate the gift of your newborn child!

Dear God, thank you for everything! Thank you for working with me to bring forth my dear little child. Thank you for giving me firsthand experience of a miracle. Thank you for giving me everyone who helped me through birth. Thank you for family and friends who help me celebrate now and who will help me take good care of our baby as the years go by. In Jesus' name, Amen.

✦ How did birth go? What were the grace moments? What were the trying times? What is most wonderful about your baby?

"The snares of death encompassed me; the pangs of Sheol laid hold on me; I suffered distress and anguish. Then I called on the name of the Lord: 'O Lord, I pray, save my life!' . . . The Lord protects the simple; when I was brought low, he saved me. Return, O my soul, to your rest, for the Lord has dealt bountifully with you."
—Psalm 116:3-4, 6-7

What a relief: you made it through! Maybe labor and delivery went more smoothly than you imagined possible. The first time I gave birth vaginally was like that. Half an hour later, I was already looking forward to doing it all again—just for the sheer intensity and thrill of it. I mentioned that fact at a women's retreat once, and an older woman looked at me as if I had lost my mind. She remembered her own labor as a long and painful ordeal. Her daughter had recently undergone a difficult and dangerous labor. Experiences of childbirth vary a lot.

Even if your labor was quick and easy, you probably feel relieved that none of your worst-case scenarios ever materialized. On the other hand, you may have had some dangerous moments. You may have had to make difficult decisions. If so, you may well feel like the psalmist quoted above—grateful to have escaped the snares of death. Perhaps you have mixed feelings—still aglow with the euphoria of giving birth but also painfully aware of the blood, sweat, and tears that went into it.

However you feel, take a moment to thank God for helping you and your baby through the uncertainties and dangers of birth. Thank God for giving you the strength to live through your distress. Thank God that you were not tested beyond what you could bear. Looking back on my own birthgiving, I can see that relief was just around the corner precisely at the point I thought I could not bear any more. To use the psalmist's words:

When I was brought low, God saved me. Remember to thank God for specific things that helped you through—a nurse taking time to comfort and encourage you, your husband bringing you ice chips and holding your hand, your doctor's skill, your midwife's wisdom, your pastor's prayers, the flow and timing of your labor. Thank God for it all!

After you have thanked God for seeing you through this birth, ask God to heal your birthing wounds. Ask God to knit those flabby muscles back together again, and to mend any tears or cuts. If you delivered your baby by cesarean section, ask God to speed your recovery from the surgery and to help you deal with the pain and discomfort.

Ask God to heal birthing wounds to your soul, too. If your plans to give birth naturally didn't work out, you may feel cheated or inadequate. If the hospital staff was impersonal and focused more on their machines than on you, you may feel strangely let down and disappointed. If you ended up having a cesarean, you may feel angry and betrayed. If your baby did not come out perfectly healthy, you may be carrying a burden of guilt and worry and grief.

Whatever your wounds, take them to God in prayer. Ask God to help you forgive yourself and others for things that went wrong. We do live in a sinful world. People do not always show wisdom and compassion. Looking into our own hearts, we know that we are not always as smart, strong, and faithful as we would like to be.

On the other hand, maybe no one was at fault for things that didn't go quite right. No matter how hard we prepare and plan, we can't completely control how birth unfolds. Going through childbirth reminds us that we are a part of nature; and nature remains powerful and unruly, in spite of human attempts to control it. Ask God to help you to learn and grow from your disappointments as well as to celebrate and draw strength from your joys and triumphs.

The joy of holding your baby in your arms has probably

already begun to heal any wounds childbirth may have left on your body or soul. The forces of nature that seemed ready to overpower you such a short while ago have ebbed away for the time being. The God who protected you and your baby through that turmoil will protect and help you through whatever challenges life may have in store. God will stay with you in the weeks ahead as you learn to interpret your baby's cries. God will stay with you when you send your little one off to school for the first time and when you try to live gracefully with a teenager's moods. God will stay with you during sickness and health, and give you the grace and confidence to live fully through it all. So, to quote the psalmist, "Return, O my soul, to your rest, for the Lord has dealt bountifully with you!"

Dear God, thank you for bringing my baby and me safely through the passage of childbirth. Heal my body and soul, and strengthen me to face whatever life brings. In Jesus' name. Amen.

✦ How do you feel about your birth experience? What wounds did you endure? What blessings did you receive?

"If we live, we live to the Lord, and if we die, we die to the Lord; so then, whether we live or whether we die, we are the Lord's. For to this end Christ died and lived again, so that he might be Lord of both the dead and the living."
—Romans 14:8 f.

We all hope it won't happen. We hope our baby will be born healthy and bright. We listen anxiously for our newborn's first vigorous cry of life, but that healthy cry doesn't always come. Some babies are born weak and must struggle for their very life. A few don't live to see their parents' faces or wriggle their tiny toes in the air.

Giving birth brings one close to death—whether or not your life was ever in danger, whether or not your baby lives. Mother and theologian Penelope Washbourn once wrote that "giving birth is as close to dying as any other human experience." In both cases the impersonal forces of nature take over. In both cases we face our limits. We find that we cannot completely control even our own bodies. We realize that we cannot guarantee a happy outcome. Still, when birth ends in death we are caught off guard. It seems so unnatural. Perhaps we are spoiled, but in our day and age we don't expect babies to die. We expect them to live and grow and eventually replace their elders.

Perhaps your baby is alive but not well. If so, you may be struggling to accept your baby's burdens. You may wonder why this happened to you and your baby. You may wonder if you can rise to the challenge of caring for your child's special needs. You may grieve for yourself and for your child. All of these feelings are perfectly normal. Pray about them and share them with people you trust. God will help you manage. Things may look bleak right now, but I suspect that God will surprise you with unimagined blessings as you care for the frail child entrusted to your care. God bless you as you begin your new life together.

Perhaps your baby's life still hangs in the balance. My prayers are with you if your baby lies in an incubator, fighting for life in the midst of tubes and machines. Modern medical technology gives underweight and premature babies a chance at life that they would not otherwise have. It can also put parents in a new kind of limbo. You may face choices that your grandparents never imagined. Watching a frail little baby struggle on and on to survive can be so hard. If your baby's slim chances of survival depend on many surgeries or other painful treatments, you may need much prayer to decide what you believe to be the most loving course of action. God bless you and your counselors as you watch and pray and make decisions on behalf of your child.

Perhaps your baby didn't survive. If so, my heart goes out to you as you mourn. Your grief at your loss is real and important. You mourn your child, even if you knew him or her only through its movements within you. You mourn your hopes and dreams. You mourn the chance to help this bud of a child blossom into adulthood. For a while, everything will remind you of your loss—the empty crib and the little clothes you so carefully gathered, the sagging belly muscles that used to hold your baby. You may feel like bursting into tears whenever you see a new mother fussing over her infant.

You will need time to lay to rest the hopes and dreams you had for this child. Give yourself time and the opportunity to mourn. Ask your pastor to conduct a funeral or memorial service for your child. Such a service gives your family and friends a chance to gather and show their support. It gives you a chance to say good-bye and to mark the passing of a brief life that you will never completely forget.

When you gather to bless your child's memory, you will hear biblical words that have comforted Christians throughout the generations. The Bible's promises can help you entrust your child to God's loving care. As the apostle Paul writes, "Whether we live or whether we die, we are the Lord's . . . Christ died and lived again, so that he might be Lord of both the dead and the living." Your separation from your child is not forever. In ways we can only begin to imagine, you and your child are united in Christ. Moreover, as you struggle to come to terms with your grief, remember that God, too, knows how it feels to lose a child. God knows how you suffer. God can take your anguish and your anger. God will help you live through the darkest night of the soul, so don't be afraid to pour out your heart in prayer.

Childbirth draws each of us into the mysteries of life and death—some more deeply than others. Whatever your sorrows, whatever your regrets about the past or your concerns about the future, take comfort and hope from Christ who is Lord of both the dead and the living. Take heart, for as Paul writes in Romans 8, ". . . in everything God works for good with those who love God."

Dear God, help me live through my sorrow. I don't understand why things couldn't have turned out more happily. I'm hurt and angry and confused and scared. Help me trust you even when things go wrong. Thank you for helping me through these hard times. Thank you for the people who love and care for me. Most of all, thank you for giving your Son and for the promise of eternal life. Amen.

✦ How has childbirth drawn you into the mysteries of life and death?

"And all who heard it were amazed at what the shepherds told them. But Mary treasured all these words and pondered them in her mind."
—Luke 2:18-19

Sharon was still glowing when I visited her in the hospital maternity ward. She sat propped up in her bed, waiting for a nurse to bring in her newborn for nursing. "How did it go?" I asked.

"Have you ever given birth?" I shook my head. I was still a student at the time, and not yet a mother. "Well," Sharon said dreamily, "then I don't think I can really explain it."

Giving birth does leave most of us groping for words. The

events are so dramatic. The physical sensations and the emotions are so intense. The mysteries of life and death are so close at hand. How can words capture it all?

Still, most of us try. When people ask, we tell how long we labored and how much the baby weighed. We may tell about what we were doing when labor started and how we got to the hospital. We tell about the ordeal we went through. We tell about our joy and wonder at the sight of our baby.

Telling birth stories is an age-old practice. You can read birth stories that are centuries old in the Bible. The story of Jesus' birth is by far the most detailed and extraordinary among them. As we hear every Christmas, Mary had plenty to keep and ponder in her heart! The Bible contains stories about less famous births, too. Genesis 25 tells the birth story of Rebekah's twins. Genesis 35 tells of Rachel's hard labor. Elsewhere you can glimpse birth stories through the name a mother chooses for her child. Eve names her firstborn Cain, because Cain sounds like the Hebrew word that means create or produce. You can just hear Eve's joy and sense of accomplishment! The birth story you can read between the lines of 1 Chronicles 4:9 sounds like more of an ordeal. There a woman names her son Jabez because the name sounds like the Hebrew word for sorrow or travail.

Try to find time to reflect on your birth story. I know this is a busy time for you, as you get acquainted with your baby and learn to respond to its needs. Perhaps you can find time to meditate quietly while nursing your baby. Perhaps you tend rather to think and reflect in the midst of telling your story to family and friends. In any case, think about how you felt. Go over the turning points in your labor. Look for God's hand in it all.

Start by thinking about how your labor started. Maybe your first contractions woke you up in the middle of the night. Maybe you noticed them while in the midst of your daily routine. Maybe labor started dramatically, with a gush of amniotic fluid. Maybe it began so gradually that you can't pinpoint the actual start. I know a woman who couldn't figure out why she had such a hard time finding a comfortable position in the pew—until she realized she was well on her way to giving birth to her third child! Where were you? Did you know for sure what was happening? How did you feel: Did you rush to the hospital or send for the midwife, or did you try to put it off? Were you calm or excited, worried or relieved, or some other mix of emotions?

Go on to think about labor itself. Who was on hand to help you? Was labor long or short? If you were hooked up to various medical machines, think about how that felt. Shiny machines give some women a sense of security. They make others feel trapped and dependent. Still others put up with it and try to make the best of it. Take the fetal monitor that churned out yards of paper as we waited for my contractions to get moving. When a nurse came in to load more paper, my husband asked her if we could have a scrap of the printout for a souvenir. "Sorry, that's against hospital policy," the nurse said—and then gave us a little piece anyway. Remember those funny little incidents and human touches in a sterile world. They are part of the story your children will love to hear when they are old enough to understand.

Think about what surprised you most. Think about what went through your mind and what people said to you. Think about the obstacles you had to overcome and the blessings that helped you through. Were there moments when you came close to despair? Were there moments when your faith saw you through? Were there moments of sheer grace? Remember the prayers you said and the decisions you had to make. Think about what it felt like to push, and what your first thoughts and feelings were when you saw your baby for the first time. Remember it all, and ask your husband or labor companion to add their impressions.

You may want to jot a few thoughts down in your baby book. Surely the way you felt giving birth is as important as your baby's length and weight! In any case, savor your story. Tell it to those who will listen. Celebrate the miracle of your child's birth!

Dear God, thank you for including me in the miracle of birth. Thank you for giving me words to express my feelings and tell my story. Help me see your hand in my life. Help me share your presence with those around me. Amen.

✦ What did you think and feel as you gave birth? What surprised you most about childbirth?

"Then suddenly a woman who had been suffering hemorrhages for twelve years came up behind him and touched the fringe of his cloak, for she said to herself, 'If I only touch his cloak, I will be made well.' Jesus turned, and seeing her he said, 'Take heart, daughter; your faith has made you well.'"
—Matthew 9:20-22

The first euphoric hours and days are past. Those few pampered days in the hospital are just a memory. Hospital food is rarely a gourmet treat, but at least you don't have to cook it yourself. Hospital beds and around-the-clock activity get old after a while, but you can always send your baby to the nursery for a few hours if you need to sleep.

Entering the foreign world of the hospital may have been a shock to your system. Coming home may be a shock, too—perhaps much more so than you expected. If this is your first child, you may feel alone and a little uncertain: "Bathing baby seemed to go so effortlessly for the nurse. Why does he scream so when I try?" If you've been through this before, you probably don't have to worry about how to change a diaper. On the other hand, you may feel overwhelmed by all the new needs you have to juggle. Older children will have missed you while you were gone and want your attention once you come home. They may well need extra loving now that an attention-grabbing newcomer has come into their world.

Then there's your body. The belly that was so round and ripe and firm a few weeks ago looks deflated and slack now. No wonder you may feel a little depressed some days. When you give birth, you win something and you lose something. You gain a child to hold in your arms, but you lose part of your pregnant body. Indeed, your pregnant self "dies" when you give birth. It probably took you a while to get used to being pregnant. So, too, it will take a while to say good-bye to your pregnant self. It will take a while for your body to heal and get back into shape.

Take heart; deep inside you the healing has already begun. Little by little your uterus is returning to its non-pregnant size. Little by little your insides heal and the bleeding will stop. Listen to your body and give it time to heal. Help your body along with gentle exercises to tone your muscles, but don't push too hard.

The Bible has some good advice on this point, although you have to dig a little to get at it. In fact, you have to dig through a pile of rules about the "uncleanness" said to follow childbirth. (You can find them in Leviticus 12.) The whole idea of uncleanness sounds strange and even insulting to modern ears. Even so, these rules served a valuable function for Hebrew women. They gave women a kind of maternity leave. Women who were "unclean" due to the flow of menstrual or birthing blood had to stay out of the daily hustle and bustle. A new mother stayed secluded with her baby in the birthing hut for the first week or two of its life. After that, mother and child could go back into household life, but they did not go out in public. Six to twelve weeks after birth, the mother was ready to participate in public life once again. The weeks of staying home ended with a festive trip to the temple.

I was amazed to note how well the Bible reflected the rhythms of the childbearing woman's body. Six weeks after the birth of your baby, your uterus should be back to its normal size and your bleeding should have stopped. Perhaps that is the reason that maternity leaves in the United States today are often set at six weeks. Take a tip from the Bible—keep life as simple as you can during the first several weeks. Let people help you when they offer. Keep meals simple or call out for pizza. Ignore the mess. Stay home and relax as much as you can. As you may have discovered, trips that once were quick and easy become major undertakings for a newborn family. I'll never forget the first time my husband and I went to church after the birth of our first child. We bustled around the apartment, getting washed and dressed, feeding the baby, and packing the diaper bag. Finally we were all ready, and got into the car. Moments later we heard sounds of life from the car seat—so I spent the ride to church changing diapers and cleaning up baby once again!

Rather than pushing yourself too hard and too fast, take the time you need. Use the time to let your body heal and your spirit catch up with the big changes in your body and your life. Use the time to get acquainted with your baby.

And when you are ready to get back into the swing of things, celebrate it! Tell your pastor when you plan to come back to church for the first time after your child's birth. Ask him or her to include special prayers for you. (You can find ideas for a simple ceremony during worship in my first book, *Giving Birth: Reclaiming Biblical Metaphor for Pastoral Practice.* See the bibliography at the back of this book.)

Give yourself time. Share your ups and downs with those who love you, and ask for help when you need it. God will bless and heal you. Your body will get back into shape. Your bleeding will taper off and stop. As Jesus said to the woman who touched his cloak for healing, "Take heart daughter, your faith has made you well."

Dear God, thank you for helping me give birth. Thank you for my baby and all my family. Thank you for healing my body and for strengthening my soul. Give me the wisdom and grace to live happily in this new chapter of my life. Amen.

✦ How do you feel about your life now? Where do you see your greatest need for help and healing?

***"He will not let your foot be moved;
he who keeps you will not slumber. He who keeps
Israel will neither slumber nor sleep."
—Psalm 121:3-4***

The first few weeks after birth always felt like chaos to me—day and night turned upside down. I'd be up in the night feeding and quieting a hungry baby. The next day I'd try to catch some sleep whenever I could. For a while life seemed like a blur of feedings and changings and naps.

Newborns do tend to be more active at night than during the day. It takes a while for them to change habits formed in the womb. While your baby was still inside you, your daytime activities would gently rock baby to sleep. When you settled down at night, the gymnastics could begin inside you. Don't be surprised if your baby takes a few weeks to get used to a new routine.

How have you been managing? Maybe you surprise yourself with how well you have been rolling with the punches. Many of us find we have energy reserves we didn't know we had. Somehow we manage to crawl out of bed to answer baby's call.

Perhaps you have had help managing the chaos. Your husband

may have been able to take some time off around the baby's birth. I remember my husband walking up and down our hallway, gently lulling our baby to sleep on his shoulder. Your husband, too, may have watched the baby so you could get some rest. Fathers often enjoy such time alone with their newborn children. They need a chance to get acquainted, too.

Your mother or mother-in-law may have come to help. Sometimes this works out well; sometimes it adds new tensions. Receive such help as graciously as you can. Your child's birth may give you a chance to form new bonds with one another. At the same time, remember that you and your husband have started a new family. Your helpers have come to help—not to take over. Speak openly with them if you need more space to develop your own style of mothering. You gave birth to this baby, and you and the baby's father bear the responsibility of caring for it and guiding it as it grows. You can do it. Getting the hang of it may take a little time, but you will learn.

Perhaps you have received help from friends, coworkers, or fellow church members. A friend's casserole and salad never tasted better! A good square meal can't chase the chaos completely away, but it certainly lifts the spirits.

Perhaps you feel alone and overwhelmed. Many of us have days when we feel tired, discouraged, and alone. On days like that, I like to think of Psalm 121. The psalmist's words are so encouraging and comforting: God will not let your foot be moved; the God who keeps you will not slumber. You and I may doze off as we nurse our children in the middle of the night, but God never dozes off. God stays awake to watch and protect us. I may not be strong enough and wise enough to do everything right, but God keeps me on track with help and wisdom around the clock.

If I were a musician, I would make this verse into a lullaby. We can sing our children to sleep, confident that God will bring them safely through the night. You can fall asleep yourself, confident that God will watch over you and wake you if your baby needs you.

The sleepless nights and chaos won't last forever. One day soon you will wake up in the morning and realize that you have slept through the night. You can't beat that first good night's sleep! Weeks of waking at all hours are good for something after all: They sure help one appreciate life's simple pleasures. Over time life will slowly settle into new routines, and the chaos swirling around you now will soon fade into a blur.

In the meantime, take your odd hours as a chance to see life from a new angle. Savor those peaceful midnight moments when your baby has finally settled down at your breast. Drink in your child's hungry sucking, her little fingers grasping yours, his look of contentment when he finishes eating. As you wearily pace and pat, and hope for a burp, think of our God who never slumbers. God will keep you on track and give you energy to get through this and every trial life may bring. When you tiptoe in to check on your sleeping baby, take a moment to marvel at the miracle that wakes you in the night and keeps you so busy during the day. Take a moment to thank God for guarding you and your baby while you sleep. Thank God for blowing into your life with new challenges and new delights.

Dear God, thank you for the simple things in life. Thank you for our baby. Thank you for food to eat, work to do, and time to rest. Thank you for those who have helped me get used to life with a new baby. Thank you for faithfully watching and protecting us all. In Jesus' name, Amen.

✦ When have you felt God's presence most strongly in recent days and weeks? How do you handle less sleep and more chaos?

"Praise the Lord! Praise the Lord from the heavens; praise him in the heights! Praise him, all angels; praise him, all his host! Kings of earth and all peoples, princes and all rulers of the earth! Young men and women alike, old and young together! Let them praise the name of he Lord!"
—Psalm 148:1 f., 11-13

Praise God, you clamoring infants! Praise God, you beaming parents! Praise God, big sisters and brothers! Praise God, doting grandparents and friends! Praise God for the miracle that started so many months ago. Praise God for this new member of the human chorus!

The first several weeks and months you and your baby will have cause for much celebration. You have probably already celebrated baby's one week birthday. Perhaps you have celebrated his one month birthday, too. Little by little the features and personality of this new little world citizen begin to unfold. You, your husband, your family, and your friends may already have begun finding great family resemblances in that little baby face. Maybe your baby is as bald as your husband's baby pictures. Maybe she has a thick head of hair like yours. Maybe you see your mother's features or the shape of your father-in-law's head. You may all agree the he could become a great pianist with such elegant long fingers or an opera singer with such strong vocal cords!

Your baby stays awake and alert for longer periods of time now, too. Perhaps he or she has even cracked her first true smile. Again a chance to celebrate: what a world of difference that smile makes! He responds to you. She laughs at the silly faces and sounds you make. Older siblings quickly catch on to baby's new tricks. No longer is little sister or brother just a boring lump of baby. Suddenly he or she becomes a responsive audience and a budding playmate!

I probably don't need to tell you to rejoice in every new accomplishment. Most parents revel in each new skill their baby masters. You probably are listening eagerly for first words and watching as baby begins to get control of its big wobbly head. As the months pass, you'll watch in wonder as baby learns to turn over and then creep. Before you know it she will be crawling and climbing. Each new milestone gives you new reason to celebrate and to praise God for the continuing miracle of unfolding life.

Praise God for your child. He or she is as special and wondrous to you as any prince or princess is to his royal parents. The miracle of birth touches all of us, rich or poor, famous or not. Praise God for bringing your child safely into the world. Praise God for the talents and personality already beginning to blossom forth in your baby's miniature ways. Pray that you may wisely guide and joyfully care for the child God has given you. You have so much to enjoy and thank God for. As one older woman said as she helped me get settled for a potluck dinner amid high chair, diaper bag, toddler hanging onto my skirt and infant hanging on my shoulder, "Children are a blessing from the Lord." She was right. Some days they may drive you to distraction, but you wouldn't trade them for the world.

"Children are a blessing from the Lord," so we praise God for them. We ask God to help us raise them to be the strong and caring people they are meant to be. We find ways to return them to God. We celebrate their baptism and welcome them into God's family. We teach them to pray. We share and encourage their wonder as they begin to explore the magnificent world God has created. We try to respond to their questions and pass on our knowledge and our faith. We teach them to sing and dance, and do what we can to pass the praise on!

So praise God and pass the diapers! You have lived through the adventure of pregnancy. You have started on your way through the adventure of parenthood. The best is yet to come, so shout it out: Praise God—boys and girls, mamas and papas; praise God—old and young, rich and poor; praise God—puppies and pollywogs, lions and whales, angels and insects! Praise God, all you creatures!

✦ Sing a song of all the things you want to thank and praise God for. Hallelujah! Amen!

Acknowledgments

This book owes much to the inspiration and interest of my family. My husband, Jørgen, continues to encourage and promote my work. His support makes it possible for me to mull things over and write. Moreover, his insightful reading of my manuscript and constructive criticism contributed much to the finished product. Our children, Anna, Niels, and Sophia, have lent me their stories and offered their enthusiasm and advice. They have also put up with their mom sitting behind the computer more often than they would like. My parents, Marian and Roland Hammer, have given me a sound foundation and lifelong encouragement and help.

This book has also benefitted from the stories and wisdom of many persons whose names cannot be listed here. Indeed, the book began to take shape in my mind when a mother of four mentioned that she had come up empty-handed while trying to find a good devotional book for pregnant women. Moreover, the meditations in this book have incorporated many of the anecdotes and insights people have shared with me over the years.

Finally, this book has benefitted from the commitment of the people at Augsburg Fortress Publishers. Ronald Klug showed interest in the project right from the start and ably steered the project through to completion. Alice Peppler gave me helpful comments regarding style.

To all of you, my heartfelt thanks.

MARGARET L. HAMMER

Suggested Reading

These books will give you more information on many of the topics touched on in this book's meditations.

Hammer, Margaret L. *Giving Birth: Reclaiming Biblical Metaphor for Pastoral Practice.* (Louisville: Westminster John Knox, 1994.) This book contains a thorough study of the biblical passages that picture God as mother and those that deal with childbirth. It explores the church's history regarding childbearing and suggests ways congregations can minister to childbearing families today.

Harpur, Tom. *The Uncommon Touch: An Investigation of Spiritual Healing.* (Toronto: McClelland and Stewart, 1995.) Harpur is a pastor and journalist who investigates the evidence for various forms of spiritual healing, including careful scientific research into the healing power of prayer. The book is stimulating and very readable.

Kitzinger, Sheila. *The Complete Book of Pregnancy and Childbirth.* Revised and expanded edition. (New York: Knopf, 1996.) Kitzinger is a well known and very experienced childbirth educator. This book describes what happens in pregnancy and childbirth, and provides a wealth of practical information.

Kitzinger, Sheila. *The Experience of Breastfeeding.* (New York: Penguin Books, 1980.) This introduction to breastfeeding provides balanced insights that can help you decide whether to breastfeed and practical information that will help you get off to a good start.

Klug, Lyn, ed. *Soul Weavings: A Gathering of Women's Prayers.* (Minneapolis: Augsburg, 1996.) The prayers in this book come from women around the world and over the centuries. They contain many refreshing approaches to God.

Klug, Ronald. *How to Keep a Spiritual Journal: A Guide to Journal Keeping for Inner Growth and Personal Discovery.* (Minneapolis: Augsburg, 1993.) The author provides helpful ideas for starting and keeping up a personal spiritual journal.

Nilsson, Lennart. *A Child is Born.* (New York: Delacorte Press/ Seymour Lawrence, 1990.) I recommend this book for its beautiful photographs of babies in their mother's womb. The accompanying text is also informative and well written. The book helps one see and appreciate the wonder of human birth.

Noble, Elizabeth. *Essential Exercises for the Childbearing Year: A Guide to Health and Comfort Before and After Your Baby Is Born.* (Boston: Houghton Mifflin, 1995.) Noble explains how pregnancy affects your muscles and sets forth simple exercises to help you care for them during and after birth. She also offers advice on posture, breathing, and relaxation.

Sateren, Shelley Swanson. *Miracle in My Arms: Prayers for a New Mother.* (Minneapolis: Augsburg, 1995.) These prayers are drawn from the spiritual journal which the author kept during the first year of her baby's life.

Tengbom, Mildred. *Bible Readings for Mothers.* (Minneapolis: Augsburg, 1996.) Tengbom's Bible-based devotions are down-to-earth and readable. She also includes thoughtful questions for reflection.